SEARCHING
HEART &
SCRIPTURE

with *The Gospel of John Cowboy Style*

MEL HOOTEN AND KAREN HOOTEN

WestBow
PRESS®
A DIVISION OF THOMAS NELSON
& ZONDERVAN

Scripture taken from the NEW AMERICAN STANDARD BIBLE®, Copyright © 1960, 1962, 1963, 1968, 1971, 1972, 1973, 1975, 1977, 1995 by The Lockman Foundation. Used by permission.

Scripture text is taken from "The Gospel of John Cowboy Style A Paraphrase of the Gospel in Cowboy Language" published by Westbow Press 2016.

This book is a work of non-fiction. Unless otherwise noted, the author and the publisher make no explicit guarantees as to the accuracy of the information contained in this book and in some cases, names of people and places have been altered to protect their privacy.

WestBow Press books may be ordered through booksellers or by contacting:

WestBow Press
A Division of Thomas Nelson & Zondervan
1663 Liberty Drive
Bloomington, IN 47403
www.westbowpress.com
1 (866) 928-1240

ISBN: 978-1-5127-9415-1 (sc)

Print information available on the last page.

WestBow Press rev. date: 09/23/2017

Contents

Dedication

We dedicate this book to three godly men who have been a constant support and encouragement throughout the three-year process of writing and editing this study guide, *Searching Heart & Scripture with The Gospel of John Cowboy Style*. These men served as Elders in the Cowboy Church of Tarrant County in its early years and their friendship has been of immeasurable value both personally and in ministry.

Ken Havard
Jay Paton
Joe Clements

Without them, this Study guide could never have been completed and placed in the hands of those seeking in a simple language a better and clearer understanding of the Gospel of John.

Preface

Searching Heart & Scripture began as a Tuesday night Bible study at the Cowboy Church of Tarrant County in Keller, Texas. Pastor Mel and Karen Hooten searched for culturally relevant Bible study material for cowboy churches. Finding limited resources, they decided to develop their own by translating the Gospel of John into cowboy language as a paraphrase. Along with that, Karen began devising *Thinking Questions* to aid in the study of the Gospel of John and how it ties together with all Scripture. This study guide is a result of that Bible study.

Many thanks go to that small Bible study group who faithfully spurred on the authors to keep at the task of translating John into cowboy language and developing a study guide. It started as a an attempt to provide relevant Bible study material fitting for Cowboy Church and over time grew into a project that can be used by many Western Heritage and Country Churches.

This study guide uses as its text *The Gospel of John Cowboy Style, a Paraphrase of the Gospel in Cowboy Language* by Mel Hooten. It is published by Westbow Press. The Gospel of John Cowboy Style is neither a scholarly translation nor a literal translation from original languages or from any original text or version. It is simply a rewording of Scripture in a language style suitable to the way cowboys and cowgirls might speak to one another.

It is the authors' prayer that by reading and studying the Gospel of John with the aid of *Searching Heart & Scripture* that many cowboys and cowgirls as well as others will hear God's voice and join Him as their riding partner on the trail of life. And if you do join Him on that trail, hang on to the pommel of your saddle because it will be the most exciting and exhilarating trail ride of your life.

Large portions of *Searching Heart & Scripture* (Those portions exceeding one chapter in length) cannot be copied or reproduced without the authors consent or permission.

Authors Mel and Karen Hooten
Searching Heart & Scripture
2017

*Note that throughout *The Gospel of John Cowboy Style a Paraphrase of the Gospel in Cowboy Language*, the words of Christ are in *Italics*. Personal pronouns relating to God the Father, Son, and Holy Spirit are capitalized in recognition of deity.

How To Use This Study Guide

Searching Heart & Scripture is designed to be used as a group Bible study of the Gospel of John or as an individual study. Either way *Searching Heart & Scripture* is a study guide that will allow students to dig deeper and come away with a better understanding of the message of this most beloved Gospel.

When used as a group Bible study, it is suggested that each participant purchase his/her own workbook. Sessions are best taught when students can come to the study having already read through the Scriptures and examined the *Thinking Questions* prior to the group discussion. Answers to some of the Thinking Questions will be deeply personal and each student will want to keep those in his/her notebook for future reference.

An ideal size for a weekly Bible Study group is 8 – 12 students. This will provide each person an opportunity to participate in the discussion. It is suggested that each small Bible study group will have one facilitator who will keep the discussion relevant to the study and on track. The facilitator for the study may be appointed beforehand (such as an elder, teacher or pastor) or a mature Christian with a good grasp of Scripture may be chosen at the first meeting of the study group. Individual participation within the group is highly recommended.

A weekend study with a larger group might be taught by the pastor, an elder, a gifted teacher or someone from outside invited to teach the study. It is recommended that the teacher complete the Bible study and become familiar with the contents and answers to the *Thinking Questions* before attempting to teach in a weekend Bible study. A leader's document with study question answers and commentary is available by email from the author by contacting mel.pardner@yahoo.com. The following schedule is recommended for a weekend Bible Study:

- Friday Evening
  6:00 (pot-luck dinner)
  7:00 – 9:00 (Bible Study with one break)
- Saturday
  8:00 (continental breakfast – donuts, fruit, coffee, juice, etc.)
  9:00 – 12:00 (Bible Study with one break)
  12:00 (lunch break – sandwiches)
  1:00 – 4:30 (Bible Study with two breaks)
  4:30 – 7:00 (Break – Students on their own for supper)
  7:00 – 9:00 (Bible Study with one break)
- Sunday Morning
  9:30 – 10:30 (Bible Study)
  11:00 – 12:00 (concluding Bible Study during worship service)

*Note: If *Searching Heart & Scripture* is used as a weekend study with a large group, some of the material will necessarily need to be summarized and abbreviated. Parts of the study likely will be left out. (The entire study, however can be completed by students in their personal time). In a large group setting, individual discussion and participation may be enhanced by seating at multiple round tables.

When *Searching Heart & Scripture* is used as an individual Bible study, it is recommended that a regular time and place be set aside. No more than one or two lessons daily is best with time to pray. Be honest with your answers to the *Thinking Questions*, spend quiet moments with the Lord and allow Him to speak to you. It may be that you will want to share some of your insights gained from the study of John's Gospel with a trusted friend who will rejoice with you in your growing faith and deepening knowledge of God's Word.

Whether in a group setting or as a study on your own, allow the Holy Spirit to be your guide. It is the prayer of the authors that God will richly enrich your life though the Study of the Gospel of john with the aid of *Searching Heart & Scripture.*

Text in the *Searching Heart & Scripture* workbook is *The Gospel of John in Cowboy Language.* It is recommended that authorized versions and/or translations be used along with that paraphrase. Translations and versions recommended are the King James Version, American Standard Version Updated edition, English Standard Version, New King James Version, the Holman Christian Standard Bible, and the New International Version.

Introduction

Cowboys and cowgirls know that working with livestock is a big job. Whether you are in rodeo or working cattle or horses on a ranch it's big work. Having the right gear and equipment and tools to do the work is mighty important for the tasks to get done.

That's true for a lot of folks in a variety of endeavors. It's also true for the big work that Jesus has given us to do as His hands in building the kingdom of God and caring for those He calls His own.

Ask any bull rider what he will need before he climbs onto that massive beast. He will give you a very specific list of items such as a well-resined bull rope, chaps, and a tough leather glove. The bronc rider and the steer wrestler can tell you what gear they have found to be most important. A barrel racer can tell you about her saddle and tack and the preparation and practice that will make the difference. To be able to compete in his or her event in the arena each cowboy and cowgirl must have the right gear and equipment.

On the range or in a corral the same is true for a ranch cowboy. He needs his saddle, leggings, a good lariat and a working knowledge of the work he has to do and what he wants to accomplish. Anything can happen. Being prepared can make all the difference.

Even more importantly, God has given us His word to equip us and prepare us for whatever we might face on the trail of life. In our own trail ride with the Lord, He gives us what we need to live our own best personal life and get the "big work" done that He has called us to. Through prayer and study of His word we can be prepared and equipped to handle what comes our way.

It is our intent that *Searching Heart & Scripture with the Gospel of John Cowboy Style* will get you saddled up for a clearer understanding of what God is saying to us through His Word. God wants to reveal Himself to us through His word so that we may know Him better. This is one way He prepares us to know how to live out His will for our lives.

We have tried to scout out some of the deep truths of the Gospel of John using thoughts and questions to guide us. It is designed to be used in a group setting with a designated leader to facilitate open discussion of Scripture. It also works well as a personal Bible study.

Scripture for this study guide is taken from *The Gospel of John Cowboy Style: A Paraphrase of the Gospel in Cowboy Language* written by Mel Hooten. A parallel reading from other Bible translations may prove to be helpful in the study of John as well.

Chapter One

Comin' To His Own

¹ Before time was ever started, Jesus was there. Jesus was with God and Jesus was surely God.

² Before ever any woods or prairies, outfits or herds, He was there. At the very first rodeo when the chute opened He was right there with God.

³ Everything as far as eye can see was made by Jesus, and without Jesus nothin' was made that has been made.

⁴ In Jesus was the spark of life, and that life is the Light for all folks.

⁵ The Light shines in the darkness and the darkness can't do anything about it.

Chapter 1 Just Thinkin

The first person we meet in the Gospel of John is Jesus. John wants us to know right away that Jesus has always existed, even from before the very beginning of time. Jesus' life didn't just begin at the time of His earthly birth in Bethlehem (the event we celebrate at Christmas). He has always existed. He is fully God and fully human. John reveals that as God, Jesus is the Creator of the universe and as God He also came to earth in flesh, fully human to live and walk on this earth and to die on the cross as the perfect substitute for our sins

Thinkin' Questions

1. What does this Scripture tell us about the origin of Jesus?

2. The Bible teaches that Jesus was *"born"* in Bethlehem. How does that figure in to Him being with God *"before time was ever started"*?

3. **Verse 3** speaks of Jesus as Creator. **Colossians 1:16-17** confirms this truth. Study these verses carefully. What words are used to describe how Jesus is involved in the created order of our world?

    1. *"All things were made _____ Him and without Him there would be _____."* **John 1:3**
    2. *"All things were created _____ Him and _____ Him."* ---- **last part of Colossians 1:16**
    3. *"He exists _____ all things and in Him all things _____ _____."* **Colossians 1:17**

4. In addition to holding His creation together, how is Jesus involved in creating things now and in the future? **Read 2 Corinthians 5:17; John 14:2-3 and Revelation 21:1.**

⁶ There once came a straight-shootin' man sent from God whose name was John (the Baptist).

⁷ He came as a fella who knows how it is, and he came to tell it plain and simple that Jesus rightly is the Light, so that everybody would know and believe.

⁸ This fella (John) was not himself the Light, but he came to tell folks about the Light.

Related Scriptures: Matthew 11:10   Mark 1:2   Luke 7:27

Thinkin' Questions

1. John, the Baptist, was sent as a messenger to the people of his day. Has God ever sent anyone to you as a messenger? Did you listen? What do you remember about it?

2. All Scripture is God's message to us. John summed up the message of the New Testament in **1 John 1:5-7 and 1 John 3:11**. Write your own thoughts about the message God wants you to deliver to others.

3. Sometimes God uses unlikely folks to do His work. Has He ever used you in a special way? Write down your experience.

Editor's note: *Through the work of the Holy Spirit, God's messengers wrote His word down for us. All other messages and messengers must be checked against the scriptures for their value. God does not contradict His Holy Word.*

[9] There is only one true Light and that's Jesus. By comin' into the world He brings the Light to us, and sure 'nough, our hearts know it's true.

[10] When Jesus was walkin' this earth which He done made with His own hands, folks didn't recognize Him for the most part. They had their own ideas.

[11] Jesus showed up to the very outfit He put together. He made these folks out of the dust and had been preparin' them since the beginning, but they did not accept Him as the Trail Boss or anything else. It was round-up time, but they weren't having any of it.

Thinkin' Questions

1. **Read 1 John 1:5-7.** What does this say about the *Light of God*? What impact does it have on our lives?

2. According to **John 3:19-21** why is it that some rejected the Son of God even when He was standing right in front of them?

3. What are some reasons we sometimes fail to recognize God's presence in our lives today?

4. How can we walk more consistently in the Light of Jesus? **Read John 8:12 and Colossians 3:12-17.**

[12] Still there were some who trusted Him. He rode right up and made them part of His fam'ly. They became His own kin, even those who just took Him at His word and believed that He was the Christ.

[13] And so they were born again, not a physical birth that has to do with flesh and blood, and not a birthin' that any man's desire had anything to do with. They were born by a spiritual birth into God's own fam'ly on account of His will alone.

[14] At the appointed time Jesus took on flesh and became a man. He lived here amongst us and lots of folks, includin' cowboys and cowgirls, saw His glory and it was a sight to behold. It was the glory of the Son of God. His grace and truth done shined forth 'cause He was plumb filled up with it.

Chapter 1 ❦❧ Just Thinkin

To help a foal bond with its owner, it is important to begin training at the very moment of its birth. Horse handlers call it "imprint training". When a horse is "imprinted" it is more likely to feel at ease with human touch and training capabilities will be enhanced. Sadly, John tells us that lots of Jewish folks whom Jesus called "His own" never bonded with Him; they were never imprinted. However there were some who did bond with Him, not by human birth or any other means, but by believing in Him by faith as the Son of God.

Thinkin' Questions

1. How old were you when you first heard of Jesus?_____

2. Did you believe right away? _____ When did you first really believe in Jesus? Write down what you remember about it . . .

3. What does it mean to you to be spiritually *"born"* as **verse 13** describes? Did you experience something that might be described in that way? Can you explain it?

4. **Read verse 14.** Explain what it means to you personally that Jesus became a man like us.

[15] John (the Baptist) called out to all the folks around. He told 'em, "He's here! ...the One I've been tellin' y'all about. He is greater than me because He existed before."

[16] For sure we've got all God's blessin' and grace right here; and more blessin' and more grace just keeps on comin'.

[17] Yes-sir-ee Moses, that Old Testament prophet gave us the Law; but now Jesus Christ has done give us grace and truth which is by a long shot better.

Thinkin' Questions

1. We know that John the Baptizer was born before Jesus, so how is it that Jesus existed before him? **Read John 8:58; Colossians 1:15-20.**

2. According to **verse 16**, how much of God do we receive in Jesus Christ? _____ **Read Ephesians 3:19.** What does this mean to you personally?

3. In your own words, what is the difference between the Law of God and the Grace of God?

¹⁸ No one on this earth has ever laid eyes on God the Father. But now Jesus, He has seen Him. Bein' His only Son, He is one with the Father and has rode in here to show Him to us.

¹⁹ Then the Jews sent some religious know-it-alls (priests and Levites) out to ask John the Baptist who he was and what he was up to.

²⁰ He fessed up and didn't deny nothin' but said it straight, "I ain't the Christ."

²¹ So they asked him, "What then? Are you Elijah?" He said, "Nope, I surely ain't." "Are you the prophet?" Again he answered, "Nope".

²² "Well, who are you then?" they demanded. "What do ya have to say fer yourself? We have to give an answer to our bosses who done sent us out here."

²³ So John replied to 'em, "'I am 'the voice of one crying in the wilderness. Make straight the way of the Lord' (Isaiah 40:3). It's just like Isaiah the Prophet did tell about."

Thinkin' Questions

1. The primary mission of Jesus was the cross. According to **verse 18**, what is another reason Christ came?

2. According to these and other Scriptures in the Bible, who was John the Baptizer? What was his purpose and relationship to Jesus? **Look it up in Luke 1:13-17; Matthew 11:7-15; also in Matthew 17:10-13.**

3. Why do you think John the Baptist said he was not Elijah?

[24] These religious know-it-alls were sent out there by a gang of other religious hot-shots who called themselves Pharisees.

[25] Them dudes pondered some more and said to him, "If you are not the Christ, nor Elijah, nor the Prophet, why in thunder are you out here baptizin'?"

[26] So John told 'em, "I baptize in water, but there is a Fella who stands amongst us that y'all ain't met yet.

[27] I ain't even worthy to unbuckle His spurs or pull off His boots for Him."

[28] Now all this that happened between John and those religious what-nots took place at a town called Bethany, just a short ride from the Jordan River where he was baptizin' a lot of folks.

Note: The Pharisees were a religious and political party in New Testament times. They lived pious, disciplined lives and were known for insisting that the law of God be observed as the scribes interpreted it and for their special commitment to tithing and ritual purity.

Thinkin' Questions

1. Why do you think the Pharisees were concerned about John, the Baptizer?

2. The Pharisees must have realized that John was claiming that the Messiah was alive and about to appear on the scene. If they were truly close to God, what do you think their attitude might have been?

²⁹ The next day John saw Jesus a'walkin' along toward him and he just shouted it out, "Behold, the Lamb of God who takes away the sin of the world!"

³⁰ "This is the Fella I've been a-tellin y'all about. You recall I said, 'After me, another Dude is comin'. He is way more than I ever thought about 'cause He existed long before me.'

³¹ The first time I saw Him, well, I wasn't for sure. So I just went on baptizin' in water like God told me. I figured we would know soon enough; everyone would have a chance to know.

³² Then, ya see, I saw the sign. The Spirit came descendin' as a dove out of heaven and lit right on Him and was a-stayin' right there.

³³ I would have never known that He was the Christ for sure 'cept for what God done told me. Ya see, when God sent me to baptize folks in the river here to prepare the way; He let me know for sure if I ever was to see the Holy Spirit comin' down like a dove and hoverin' over, or lightin' on somebody and stayin' there awhile; that's the very One who will baptize in the Holy Spirit of God.

> Chapter 1 ഏᏍᏋ Just Thinkin
> One day John the Baptist pointed Jesus out to his disciples and just plumb shouted it out all excited like, "Behold the Lamb of God who takes away the sin of the world!" This title for Jesus could sum up the whole message of the Bible: "The Lamb of God". It is also the answer to an age-old question asked in Genesis 22:7, "Where is the Lamb of God!" The answer to that question is Jesus: He is the Lamb of God; only He can take away the sin of the world.
> ഏᏍᏋ

³⁴ I want you to know that I've seen that with my own two eyes and I reckon He is the Son of God for sure."

Note: There it is, John's purpose has now been fulfilled. He has introduced the Messiah. Scripture has made it clear.

Thinkin' Questions

1. What title does John use to identify Jesus in **verse 29**? "Behold! The _____ _____ _____".

2. In **verses 31-34** John went into great detail to explain how he knew with certainty that Jesus is the Son of God. Many today still question who Jesus is. How would you explain your certainty that Jesus is the Son of God?

³⁵ Next day, ol' John was out there again with a couple of his men. He had been teachin' these fellas what he knew about the comin' Messiah.

³⁶ He looked up, ya see, and there was Jesus walkin' past at that very minute. "Look yonder!" said John. "The very Lamb of God Himself!"

³⁷ John's men (called dee-sie-puls); well they knew what "Lamb of God" meant. All those folks around there knew exactly what John was a-sayin'. They lit out after Jesus.

³⁸ Jesus knew they had taken up with Him. "Howdy," He said, and he flat-out asked 'em, "Why are y'all followin' Me?" They just said, "Rabbi (which means "Teacher") we want to know where You're bunkin'."

³⁹ Jesus said to 'em, "Come on then and I'll show you My place over yonder." It was about four o'clock in the afternoon. They went with Him and stayed there for the rest of the day.

Thinkin' Questions

"The Lamb of God" carries a sense of a one and only, once and for all identification. Learn something about that title in the following related scriptures about the early Jewish sacrificial system. **Read Exodus 12:21-24 and Leviticus 1:3-5, 10-11 & 13b.**

1. What was the purpose of sacrificing these animals? **Read Exodus 30:1, 6 & 10; also I Chronicles 6:49.**

2. Was there a higher meaning to the sacrificial rituals? **See Hebrews 9:11-12 and Psalm 51:14-17.**

3. Can the blood of goats, bulls, and sheep take away sin? **Read Hebrews 9:11-15 and Hebrews 10:1-4.**

4. What does term *"Lamb of God"* mean to you personally?

~ Close this lesson with Isaiah 53:4-7. ~

[40] One of the fellas who went home with Jesus was Andrew, Simon's brother.

[41] Now after spendin' all evenin' with Jesus, Andrew was mighty excited. He high-tailed it straight to his brother, Simon, and told him straight, "We have done found the Messiah!"

[42] Nothin' else doin', first thing the next mornin' he brought his brother to meet Jesus. "Howdy Simon," Jesus said, and He looked him straight in the eye, *"Your father, John, gave you the name Simon. But I'm givin' you a new name. From here on out, you will be called Cephas."* That's just Peter to us.

Thinkin' Questions

1. Why do you think Jesus changed Simon's name? Name some others in Scripture who received new names from the LORD? **Look up Genesis 17:5 & 15; also Genesis 35:10.**

2. What does the Bible say about each of our new names in relation to Christ? **Read Revelation 2:17 & Revelation 3:12.**

[43] The next day Jesus reckoned He would go on up to Galilee. He ran into a fella by the name of Philip along the trail. *"Howdy,"* Jesus said to him, *"Ride along with Me."*

[44] Now this here Philip hailed from Bethsaida, the same hometown as Andrew and Peter.

[45] After listenin' to Jesus for a spell Philip went off lickety-split and found his buddy, Nathanael. He said, "Ya gotta come and see. We've done found the One that ol' Moses and all the prophets been a-foretellin' about; it's Jesus of Nazareth. He's Joseph the carpenter's boy, but that ain't all He is, no-sir-ee. He's a far sight more than that."

[46] Nathanael said, "Nah, you don't think anything good can come out of Nazareth, do ya?" Philip said, "You just come see for yourself."

[47] Next thing, Jesus sees Nathanael a-ridin' up. He said, right in front of everybody, *"Now here's a man who calls it like he sees it."*

[48] Nathanael said to Jesus, "How is it that you know that about me?" Jesus said, *"I know you Nathanael. I know all about you. Weren't you kicked back under a fig tree before Philip found you? I saw you there."*

[49] Then Nathanael said to Jesus, "Teacher, You are the Son of God; You are the King of Israel."

[50] Jesus said, *"If you believe what you just said because I told you I saw you under the fig tree, well, I reckon you're gonna see a lot more amazin' things comin'."*

[51] Jesus told him, *"Nathanael, with your faith you are gonna see the sky and all heaven itself opened up, and you'll see the angels of God comin' and goin' from this earth by way of Me, the Son of Man, I like to call Myself."*

Thinkin' Questions

1. After reading the story above, how do you explain Nathanael's drastic change of attitude?

2. **Read Hebrews 11:1-12.** How is your faith? Share one or two experiences or encounters with God that have strengthened your faith.

Chapter Two

Water Changed to Wine

[1] A few days after Jesus came back from forty days hard testing in the wilderness, He rode with His pardners and some of His family out to a weddin'. Mary, His mama was there.

[2] Jesus and His new pardners, (that is His *dee-si-puls*) had all been invited to attend.

[3] The family of the couple gettin' hitched were havin' a big barbeque for the whole town. The wine, which was the favored beverage in those days, well it had plumb run out long before the celebratin' was over. Jesus' mama, Mary, came and told her Son of the urgent situation.

[4] Now Jesus had not pictured His ministry a-startin' off in this particular way. So He said to His mama, "Well, ma'am, what does this thing have to do with Me? If I do what you're gettin' at, I will be startin' down a trail with no turnin' back. I'm not so sure it's time yet."

[5] His mama just said to the hired hands, "Y'all do exactly what He tells ya."

―――――――――――

Thinkin' Questions

1. Why do you think Jesus hesitated in doing what His mother knew He could do? Who would He have checked with before opening this door to public miracles? **Read John 11:41-42 and Mark 1:35-38.**

2. What do we know about Jesus that would give us insight into His decision of what to do next? **Read the following: Matthew 14:14-20; Mark 1:40-41.**

3. **Read Luke 11:5-12** regarding prayer. How might this relate to Mary's request and the need of the wedding family?

4. In order to be like Christ, list key components that we need to have in our own decision making process? **Read Philippians 2:1-5; 1 Peter 3:8-9; James 3:17 and Romans 12:2.**

⁶ Well, it just so happened there was a half-dozen big clay water pots sittin' there empty. The folks invited to the hitchin' and barbeque had used 'em to wash up on account of their religious customs in those days. I imagine every one of 'em would hold 20 or 30 gallons.

⁷ Jesus said to the hands, *"Fill these pots with water."* So they filled 'em up to the brim.

⁸ As soon as they were done fillin' up those big pots Jesus said, *"Now dip up a ladleful out of one of the pots and take it to your foreman."*

⁹ When the foreman who was in charge of the servin' of the guests took a sip of that water what was now wine he said, "Yee-ha! I don't know where this came from but I'll take it!" (Of course the hands knew where it had come from.) Then the foreman hollered out for the groom.

¹⁰ And He said to him, "I've hired on for lots of shindigs. Every outfit serves the good wine first, but you've been a-holdin' out. I'll be dogged if you ain't gone and saved the best wine for last!"

¹¹ This was the beginning of the miracles, the signs that Jesus did here on earth to show who He was. He first showed His glory in a poor village called Cana, at a weddin' amongst His family and closest friends. His pardners saw it all and believed in Him for sure now.

Thinkin' Questions

1. In response to the predicament of Jesus' friends and family, what sort of things did Jesus use to accomplish this miracle?

2. What does this quiet miracle suggest to us about ministry? **Read Ephesians 2:10.**

¹² So Jesus rode out with His mama, brothers and sisters, and His new pardners. They rode to a town called Capernaum for a spell.

¹³ Then Jesus hit the trail on up to Jerusalem. He was a might interested in what had become of the Jewish Passover customs, a right special time for the Jews.

¹⁴ He came upon a bunch of desperados in the temple. They was sellin' and tradin' for oxen, sheep, and doves. And there were some city slickers runnin' a crooked money changin' outfit right there in God's house.

¹⁵ The big business goin' on in the church-house didn't sit too well with Jesus, bein' the Son of God and all. He fixed Himself up somethin' of a bull whip and drove 'em out of there, animals and all. He turned over the money tables and sent coins flyin' everywhere. It made quite a stir.

Thinkin' Questions

Read other gospel accounts of a similar temple incident in the last week of Jesus' earthly ministry: **Matthew 21:12-13; Mark 11:15-17; Luke 19:45-46.**

1. When does anger become sin? **Check out some other Scriptures related to anger: Mark 3:5; Matthew 5:22.**

2. Why do you think Jesus took such strong action against the practices in the temple?

3. Is there such a thing as righteous anger? Explain.

4. Jesus being angry is one thing. In light of the following Scriptures what should our attitude and actions be regarding our own anger? --**Ephesians 4:26-27 & 30-32; Colossians 3:8.**

John records the turning of water into wine as Jesus' first miracle. Jesus performed lots of miracles when He was on earth. The Gospel of John records seven:

(1) Turning water to wine—John2:1-11
(2) Healing of a boy—John 4:46-54
(3) Healing of a man by a pool—John 5:1-9
(4) Feeding of the 5000—John 6:5-13
(5) Jesus walking on water—John 6:19
(6) Healing of a blind man—John 9:1-7
(7) Rasing Lazarus from the dead—John 11:38-44

John picked out these miracles as proof that Jesus is truly God, the very Son of God. He states this in *John 20:30-31 "Now there's a whole lot more signs and miracles Jesus did when He was with His pardners that ain't wrote down in this book. But these here are a handful of 'em kept in this record so y'all might each one believe that Jesus is the Messiah, the Son of God, and by believin' you can have everlastin' life in His name."*

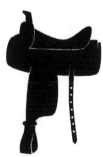

¹⁶ As for those fellas sellin' the animals for sacrifice, Jesus told them flat out, "Get all this stuff outta here now!" "You're gonna stop makin' my Father's House some kind of sale barn and money-makin' outfit!"

¹⁷ Jesus' pardners recollected that in the scriptures about the Messiah, it said, "Zeal for Your house will consume Me" (Psalm 69:9). It sure seemed to fit.

¹⁸ The hot-shot Jews in charge that day demanded, "If You think You have the authority to interfere here, then prove it!"

¹⁹ Jesus said, "Listen, y'all will tear this temple down and in three days I will raise it right on up again."

²⁰ Those fellas sputtered a bit and finally spit it out, "It took forty-six years to build this temple and You're a-sayin' You could raise it in three days?"

²¹ It didn't seem like that particular thang at the time, but Jesus was talkin' about the temple of His own body.

²² Later on when Jesus was raised from the dead, His pardners remembered the day He done made that declaration. Then they understood and believed all the Scriptures and words Jesus had spoken about Hisself.

Thinkin' Questions

1. How does Jesus' mandate in **verse 16** relate to churches today?

2. In **verses 18-22**, Jesus really didn't *"show His badge"*. Why do you think Jesus answered the religious leaders the way He did?

²³ Jesus stayed a spell in Jerusalem for that year's Passover week. It turns out lots of folks believed in Him, and they saw the signs, that is the miracles He was doin'.

²⁴ But Jesus on His part was not obligin' Himself to anybody because He knew the deep motives and thoughts of all people.

²⁵ Nobody had to tell Jesus anything about the human race. He Himself knew what was in the heart of every livin' cowboy and cowgirl and all other folks, too. And He still does to this day.

Thinkin' Questions

1. In reference to **verse 24**, how does Jesus know the deep thoughts and motives of every human being? **Read 1 Samuel 16:7.**

2. In light of the fact that our hearts are fully visible to God, how do we approach Him? **Look at James 4:6 and 1 John 1:9.**

3. How does God change us? **Read Galatians 5:22-26; Matthew 5:3-10; Philippians 4:7-8; James 3:17.**

4. Looking back on your own life, what are some changes He has made in you?

5. Read Paul's prayer for his fellow believers in **Colossians 1:9-14.** Use these Scriptures as a prayer for yourself to walk worthy of your calling in Christ.

Chapter Three

Tellin' It Like it Is

1-2 Now there was a fella, a Pharisee who they called Nicodemus, one of the big bosses of the Jews. Ol' Nicodemus came to Jesus late one night. He needed to talk real bad. He said to Jesus, "Mister, we know that God has done sent You as a teacher. Nobody can do all the miracles and stuff that You've been doin' unless God is a-makin it so."

3 Jesus said to ol' Nick, *"Listen up, 'cause here's how it is. For sure unless anybody is born again, he can't ever see heaven."*

4 Nicodemus pondered that and said, "Now how is it anybody could be borned again once they're old. He sure can't get back in his mama's womb and get borned again, can he?"

5 Jesus answered him again like this, *"I'm a-tellin you, unless a person is born of water and the Spirit, that person can never enter the Kingdom of God.*

6 *The fact of the matter is whoever is born on account of the flesh has a fleshly birthin', but whoever gets born of the Holy Spirit has a spiritual birthin'.*

Chapter 3 Just Thinkin

Every now and then a drover would find a waterin' hole or ride up on a creek or river where he could wash off the dust from the trail. Just like us he could only get the outside of his body clean. Soap n' water can't clean us up on the inside. Our thoughts, our lusts, our sinful desires can only be changed by a spiritual transformation. Jesus calls it "being born again". Ya see if we are going to heaven we're gonna have to have a second birth. The first birth is physical ("Whoever is born on account of the flesh has a fleshly birthin'")--verse 6. But the second birth is spiritual (But whoever gets born of the Spirit has a spiritual birthin'.) Only those who believe in Jesus as the Christ the Son of God can have a spiritual birth. That's what cleans us up on the inside.

7 *So don't be thrown off your horse when I say that ya must be borned again a second time.*

8 *Just like the wind blows where it wants to and you hear the sound of it, but have no understandin' of where it comes from or where it's goin'; same is true for the birthin' by the Holy Spirit of God."*

Thinkin' Questions (Use another sheet if necessary)

1. Why do you think Nicodemus came to Jesus at night?

2. Do you think the expression of being *"born again"* is understood any better today than in Nicodemus' day? How would you explain it to someone?

3. What is the significance of the *"wind"* comparison in **verse 8**? **Read Psalms 104:1-4 & Acts 2:2-4.**

⁹ Ol' Nicodemus pondered all that Jesus had said. He was scratchin' his head and sayin', "How can all this be?"

¹⁰ Jesus answered him with another question, "You say you're a teacher of Israel, the chosen people of God, and yet you don't understand what I'm tellin' ya?"

¹¹ Jesus went on to say, "We tell about what We know to be true, and We give a true account of what we've seen. Yet, it don't seem like you believe or take Our word for it.

¹² So . . . if I tell ya about earthly things and you don't believe Me, then how will you understand if I go a-tellin' you about heavenly things?

¹³ No one has gone up to heaven except one Fella. He is the One who has come down from heaven, calls Himself the Son of Man."

¹⁴⁻¹⁵ "It's like when Moses lifted up the serpent for healin' when the Hebrew children were wanderin' in the wilderness and everybody was sick and dyin'. Well, I'm a-tellin' you the Son of Man is gonna have to be lifted up like that . . . and whoever believes in Him can have life forever in heaven."

Thinkin' Questions

1. The source of Jesus' teaching and actions is:

   _____

   Read John 7:16; John 8:26, 28; John 12:49 and John 14:24.

> **Chapter 3 ℘ℭ Just Thinkin**
> The brass serpent that was lifted up in the wilderness so folks could look at it and get healed is not to be an object of superstition or an idol to worship, rather it was a symbol of faith. It pointed to the time when Jesus, the sinless Son of God would be nailed to a cross to die as the perfect substitute for our sins. Those who look to Him in faith will be saved. ℘ℭ

2. Who is "We" in **verse 11**? **Reference: John 10:30; John 17:22; Genesis 1:26.**

3. **Read** about the serpent in the wilderness in **Numbers 21:4-9**. What symbol of this event do you recognize today?

4. **Reference Jesus' words in John 12: 31-32.** What does the picture of the *serpent on a pole* represent in the life and mission of Jesus Christ?

¹⁶ "Ya see, God loves this world so much, that He gave His one and only Son to die, so that every man, woman, boy and girl who believes in Him will not die, but will be a-livin' forever.

¹⁷ God didn't send His Son into this world to judge the world at this particular time. No, but He wanted to make a way, don't ya see, for the world to be saved through the Son of God, Jesus.

¹⁸ Here's how it is for sure: Anyone that rightly believes in Jesus won't ever be judged for his sins on the final judgment day. The one who won't believe; well, he has already been judged because he or she has not believed in God's only Son.

¹⁹ Here's how they are already judged: The light came into the world, but folks bein' as they were, well, they loved the darkness more than the light 'cause their deeds were evil.

²⁰ Ya see, the folks that do evil hate the light. They won't come to the light a-fearin' their evil deeds will be shown up for everybody to see.

²¹ But on the other hand, every fella who wants to live by the true things of God, he will come to the light, 'cause he wants to know if he's got it right. He wants to do the things of God most of all."

Thinkin' Questions

1. What does Jesus mean by the term *"world"* in **verse 16?**

2. What does it mean to *"believe"* in Jesus as mentioned in **verses 16 & 18? Reflect back to some earlier verses: John 1:12-13 & John 3:3.**

3. In **verse 17,** Jesus says that He did not come to judge the world, but to save it. We know this applies to His first coming. How does this compare to Scriptures regarding His second coming? **Refer to John 5:22; Matthew 25:31-34, 41; Romans 2:16; 2 Timothy 4:1 & Revelation 19:11.**

²² It weren't long 'til Jesus and His pardners hit the trail for the territory of Judea. They camped there together for some time, baptizin' folks in the name of Jesus.

²³ John (the baptizer) was also close by. He was baptizin' lots of folks from all over the country in a place near Salim 'cause there was a lot of water. He was still doing the job that God had done give him to do.

²⁴ Ya see, ol' John hadn't been throwed in jail, yet.

²⁵ Now there was quite a ruckus that came up between John's pardners and a Jew there about the rules of what they called "Pur-ee-fee-cation" (the law of purification).

²⁶ Then John's pardners came to him and said, "Now teacher, ya know that Fella you baptized in the Jordan, the One you said you had been testifyin' about and waitin' for; well, He's baptizin' now too, and everybody is comin' to Him."

²⁷ And ol' John, he said, "Well now, that's just all right ya see. He couldn't be a-doin' that if He hadn't been given it from heaven, just like I was."

Thinkin' Questions

1. Old Testament Scripture may help us understand what the "ruckus" was about regarding purification. **Read Numbers 19:1-9 & 17-20.**

2. In **Numbers 19:6** the writer (Moses) mentions scarlet Yarn and Hyssop as two significant ingredients in the Old Testament practice of purification. What do these items symbolize? **Joshua 2:18 (the saving of Rahab). Isaiah 1:18; Matthew 27:28; Hebrews 9:19-23; Exodus 12:21-23; Psalms 51:7 and also John 19:28-30.**

3. According to **Hebrews 9:23-28** what do these things ultimately point to regarding the true and complete purification of our souls?

Note: The baptism done by John the Baptizer symbolized repentance from sin. The baptism of Jesus completes the symbolism of cleansing from sin. Our purification is now complete in Christ.

²⁸ Now you boys heard me for sure sayin' over and over, 'I ain't the Christ!' No-sir-ee, I was sent on ahead of Him.

²⁹ The fella that's gettin' hitched to the bride is called the bridegroom; but his ol' best buddy that stands up with him and hears Him a sayin' all those weddin' words, well he just gets plumb excited too, 'cause he hears his greatest friend a-talkin' about his bride. So ya see, I am just about as happy as the bridegroom himself. I'm just full to the brim, that's what I am.

³⁰ You see, this Fella Jesus; what he's a-doin' has gotta get bigger and bigger. What I'm doin' is just about done."

Thinkin' Questions

1. John must remind his disciples again what his purpose is. **Look back to: John 1:6-8; 20-23.** In your own words, what was God doing through John the Baptizer?

2. **Verse 29** references Jesus as the *"bridegroom"*. John, the Baptizer, seems to have incredible insight into the identity of Jesus. Compare to some other passages: **Matthew 9:14-15; Matthew 22:2; Matthew 25:1-12.** In what way is Jesus *"a bridegroom"*?

3. Who is the bride? **Read Ephesians 5:25-32; Revelation 19:7-9; 21:9 & Revelation 22:17.**

[31] (Then ol' John began testifyin' and prophesyin'.) He declared, "The One who comes from up yonder in heaven is higher than all the rest of us that comes from the earth. He is above everybody and everything, that's just the way it is.

[32] He tells us truly about what He has seen and heard from above; but it just seems like nobody is listenin', and they're just not understandin' what He's got to say.

[33] The ones who have believed Jesus have it settled forever in their hearts that God is true. Ya see, He's the real deal.

[34] Here's how it is: This fella Jesus who was sent from above speaks only the words of His Father. For ya see, the Father don't hold one bit of His Holy Spirit back from Him.

[35] God the Father loves His Son and has handed everythang over to Him.

[36] So anybody who believes in Jesus, the Son of God, has eternal life. That's a fact. By the same token, anybody who doesn't believe and don't take Jesus serious at all, he won't see any life beyond this 'un, but rather he will run smack dab into the wrath of God Almighty."

Thinkin' Questions

1. In **verse 31** John is saying that Jesus comes from a higher place, indeed that He is above all. **Read Isaiah 55:8-11.** Who is the One Isaiah recorded as higher in thoughts and ways? What do you think John is saying here about Jesus Christ?

2. How do we know that we have eternal life? **Read Verse 36** above. Refer back to **John 3:16**. Then look at **John 5:24 & I John 5:11-13.**

Chapter Four

An Old Waterin' Hole

¹ It weren't long 'til Jesus was a-baptizin' even more folks than ol' John the Baptist. Pretty soon, Jesus got wind that the Pharisees were in a huff about it.

² Fact of the matter is Jesus' Himself was not doin' any baptizin', but His pardners; they were baptizin' folks in His name.

³ Jesus figured it was gettin' 'bout time to move on to Galilee. So He cleared on out of Judea for the time bein'.

⁴ He was of a mind to follow the trail through Samaria, so they lit out.

⁵ He came along close to a town in Samaria called Sychar. It was located 'round the part of the country where Jacob had given a piece of land to his son Joseph a number of years back.

⁶ There was a freshwater well there that Jacob had dug with his own hands. Yes-sir-ee, Jacob's well was a known spot in that part of the world. So Jesus, being plumb tuckered out by this time, sat down by that well to rest a spell. It was right about noon.

⁷ He had no more 'n sat down before a local woman showed up to draw water. Jesus said to her, *"Howdy ma'am, I'd be much obliged if you would give Me a drink of water."*

⁸ Ya see, Jesus' pardners had done gone into town to buy some vittles and He was there all by Hisself.

⁹ Plumb bowled over, the woman says, *"Howdy, but how is it that You, being a Jew and a man, ask me for a drink on account I am a Samaritan woman?"* --Bein' how it was, Jewish folk wanted nothing at all to do with Samaritans. There was plenty of hard feelin's to go around between 'em. And a proper Jewish man would never talk to a strange woman in public, neither!

Thinkin' Questions

1. Look at **verse 2** above. What do you think was the reason Jesus was not actually doing the baptizing? **Refer to problems mentioned in the early church in 1 Corinthians 1:10-17.**

2. Jesus often decided to move on from one place of ministry to another. Sometimes trouble was brewing when it was time to move, but that was not the reason for His decision. Jesus wasn't one to back down. How did Jesus know where to go next? Who was calling the shots for Jesus' travels and encounters? **Read John 6:38; Mark 1:35-38; Luke 2:49; John 14:10-11.**

¹⁰ Jesus gave her a straight answer and it was quite a mouthful, yessir-ee. He said, *"I tell you, ma'am, if you knew that God has done sent you just what you've been prayin' for; and if you knew who it is sayin' to you, 'I'd be obliged for a drink of water', you would be askin' Him, and He would sure 'nough give you living water."*

¹¹ She said to Him, "Mister, You don't even have a bucket to draw water with and the well is deep; how do You think then, that You could get any water up for me?"

¹² She then went on to say, "Our ancestor, Jacob, gave us this well. He drank from it himself, and his boys and his cattle. Are You sayin' that You're greater than he is?

¹³ Jesus wanted her to understand. *"Folks who drink this water will get thirsty again and again,"* He said.

Chapter 4 Just Thinkin

One of America's most beloved western songs is "Cool Water". It was sung and recorded by such greats as Hank Williams, Marty Robins and Roy Rogers and Sons of the Pioneers. Written by Bob Nolan, it tells about an old prospector and his mule named Dan. In the song the prospector looks out across the burning sands and sees a pool of cool clear water, but to his disappointment it turns out only to be a mirage. The water Jesus offers the Samaritan woman at Jacob's well was not a mirage nor did it disappoint because Jesus' offer was "An everlastin' spring" of 'living water' that would take her right on through this life and the next" (John 4:14).

¹⁴ *"The water that I give has nothin' to do with this well. Anyone who drinks My water will never have to be thirsty again in his soul, like you are right now. Ya see, the water that I give will be like an everlastin' spring that will take you right on through this life and the next."*

¹⁵ Pondering this, the woman said to Him, "Yes, Sir! Give me this water so that I won't be thirsty again and won't have to come here to get the water that I need."

Thinkin' Questions

1. What is this *Living Water* that Jesus is talking about? **Read John 7:37-39 and Revelation 22:1.**

2. The Holy Spirit is often symbolized by flowing water or pools of water in Scripture. **Read Isaiah 44:3-5; Isaiah 55:1 and Isaiah 58:11. Also Read Psalm 42:1-2.** Describe in your words how the Spirit of God is like water.

3. Do you have *Living Water* flowing in your life? In **John 7:37**, the literal translation is "keep on coming and keep on drinking." Are you drinking your fill every day or are you living in drought because you do not drink? What is our responsibility as believers? **Read Revelation 21:6-7 and Revelation 22:1&17.**

¹⁶ Jesus said, "Yes ma'am, but first go and get your husband and bring him back here."

¹⁷ The woman then said, "Uh, the truth is I don't really have a husband." And Jesus said, "Yes ma'am you are talkin' the plain truth when you say that.

¹⁸ Ya see, I know that you have had five husbands. And I know that you are not married to the man you are now livin' with. You are speakin' the truth to Me and bein' honest. That is an important thing."

¹⁹ The woman then knew this was no ordinary man she was talking to. She said to Jesus, "Sir, You must a prophet."

Thinkin' Questions

1. Jesus obviously knew the woman's marital history and present situation. Why do you think He told her to go get her husband?

2. Notice how Jesus pointed out the woman's past, yet did not speak words of condemnation over her. In fact, He found something to commend her for. What was it?

3. What does this encounter teach us about talking to another person regarding his or her spiritual condition?

4. How do we approach the Lord Jesus with our past or present sin? **Read Psalms 32:5; Proverbs 28:13; 1 John 1:8-9.**

²⁰ She went on, "Our people worship God at this mountain because our pioneer forefathers worshiped here as Jacob did. But y'all Jews say that Jerusalem is the only place to rightly worship. Can You tell me for sure which is right?"

²¹ Jesus answered her like this, "Ma'am, this might be a bit hard for you to understand now, but there is comin' a time when there won't be any partic'lar place that is better than another for worshipin'.

²² Ya see, y'all have been worshipin' what you do not know. As Jews, we worship what we do rightly know because we have God's promise of salvation.

²³ But I reckon that's all about to change. The answers you seek will soon come clear to ya. See, true worshipers can worship the Father anytime and anywhere when they go a-lookin' for Him in spirit and truth. Folks like that, well, it doesn't matter where they are from. The Father searches for 'em and finds them right where they are.

²⁴ Ya see, God is Spirit. He can be any place and everywhere. When the fellas and gals who worship Him call out to Him in their hearts, honest-like and sincere, well, He'll be there. He will hear them. He has done heard you, ma'am."

Thinkin' Questions

1. What is Jesus saying to the Samaritan woman about locations for worshiping God?

2. "Worship" for me means:

3. Are there "places" that are better than others for you to worship? Explain:

4. How do we worship *"in spirit and truth"*? **Read Acts 17:24-28.**

²⁵ The woman responded, "I know I don't understand everything now, but I believe God is gonna send Messiah to us one day, the One who is the Christ. He's will make it all clear."

²⁶ Jesus then said to her, *"I am He, the very One who is speakin' to ya right now!"*

²⁷ Now Jesus pardners were comin' and could see from a long way off that Jesus was sittin' at the well talkin' to a woman. They were plumb dumbfounded as they approached. They saw her drop her water pot to the ground, and they could see that she and Jesus were havin' quite a conversation. (It looked like she bowed down at His feet.)

²⁸ Then she ran off without her water pot back to the town as fast as she could go.

²⁹ When she got to town she began tellin' all the men folk she could find, "Y'all come out to the well and meet a Man who told me everything about my life, even things no one knows about me! If this ain't the Christ, the sun ain't hot!"

³⁰ There must've been somethin' convincin' about her 'cause they were all comin' out to meet Him maybe figurin' if He knew everything about her, it just might include them.

Thinkin' Questions

1. Once a person believes that Jesus is who He says He is, what is the next step to salvation?

2. Does it appear in **verse 29** that she is now a believer in Jesus Christ as her Savior? Why do you think so?

3. Can you list evidences in your life that would convince others that you are a true believer?

³¹ Meanwhile His pardners figurin' Jesus must be starvin' were tryin' to get Him to eat some of the grub they had done brought back.

³² But Jesus said, "Aw, I'm good! Ya see, I've got vittles y'all don't know about."

³³ The pardners all looked at each other shakin' their heads. "No one had brought Him any grub, had they?"

³⁴ Then Jesus told 'em, "Fellas, My food is to do what My Pa sent Me to do. Takin' care of the job He sent Me to tend to, well that fills Me plumb up.

³⁵ Y'all look at the fields and reckon the harvest is still four months off. But I'm tellin' y'all to lift your eyes and look on another field; one that I can see. I'm tellin' ya the grain is already white and ready for harvestin'.

³⁶ Even now the fella that reaps is gettin' his wages paid, and he is gatherin' fruit for his life everlastin'. Ya see, the one who sows and the one who done comes along and reaps; well, they can both be a-grinnin' with joy over the crop.

³⁷ In this case, that old sayin' is true: One sows and another reaps.

³⁸ I sent you to reap fruit that you didn't plant. Others have labored 'fore you got here, and y'all have done partnered up with them."

Thinkin' Questions

1. What *"vittles"* do you think Jesus is referring to here in **verse 32? Check out verse 34; also John 6:38-40 and John 17:4.** Have you ever experienced this kind of "food"? _____ If not, say a prayer to ask God for spiritual food.

2. What harvest is Jesus talking about? **Read Luke 10:2.**

3. What is the fruit mentioned in **verse 36? See Matthew 13:23 & John 15:5-8.**

4. Who were the *"other planters"*? **Refer to Hebrews 1:1 & 1 Peter 1:10-12.**

³⁹ A whole herd of Samaritan folks from the little town of Sychar believed in Jesus that day because the woman spoke up sayin', "He knows all about me and everything I've done."

⁴⁰ When the Samaritan fellas found Jesus, they were much obliged for Him to stay on a spell with them and their families. And so He stayed on with 'em.

⁴¹ Jesus told them the truth of His word and lots of folks believed.

⁴² "And 'sides that," they said to the woman, "It ain't just 'cause of what you said that we believe. We done heard for ourselves and reckon that He is the One we've been lookin' for. He really is the Savior of the world!"

⁴³ Jesus stayed with those folks for a couple more days 'til every last one of 'em had a chance to find out who He was and make up his own mind. Then He hit the trail toward Galilee.

Thinkin' Questions

1. During the few days they spent in Samaria, the disciples witnessed a part of the *"great harvest"* that Jesus had mentioned in **verse 35**. What are some things they may have learned from that experience?

2. **Read Acts 8:14-17.** What now is the attitude of these Jewish Apostles towards the Samaritans?

3. Has your relationship with Jesus changed your attitude toward others who are from a different culture or race? If so, in what way?

4. Are there still old prejudices and attitudes that need to be cleansed from your heart? If so, take time right now to make this a matter of prayer.

[44] Jesus Himself declared that a prophet has no honor in the place where he comes from.

[45] When He rode into Galilee, folks there seemed to be plumb glad to see Him. Ya see, the word was out about the miracles Jesus done at the big feast in Jerusalem awhile back. A bunch of them had been there and seen and heard for themselves first hand all the things He had done.

[46] Jesus made His way back again to parts around Cana of Galilee, the place where He had turned the water to wine. There was this high up government man there whose boy was mighty sick in the nearby town of Capernaum.

[47] When that fella got wind that Jesus was back in the parts around Galilee, he went lookin' for Him. I'm tellin' ya, when he found Jesus, he got off his horse and downright begged Jesus to come back with him to heal his boy who was about to die any minute.

[48] Now Jesus, knowin' about this man and plenty of folks like him, kindly pointed out the sad fact that they have to see miracles or else they just won't believe in Him.

Thinkin' Questions

1. Why do you think Jesus is so concerned about the people's need for signs? **Read Matthew 12:38-39; Matthew 16:1-4; Matthew 24:23-25; John 2:23-25; Revelation 13:13-14 and Revelation 19:20.**

2. What do miracles have to do with why Jesus came? **Check out Mark 16:20; John 20:30-31 and Hebrews 2:4.**

3. How does the need for miracles fit with worshiping *"in spirit and truth"* spoken of in **verse 24?**

⁴⁹ But this high up government fella was plumb desperate, it was plain to see. He said, "With all respect, Sir please, won't You come before my boy dies?"

⁵⁰ So Jesus just said to Him straight out, *"I'll give you one better. You just ride on back to your house now, your boy's gonna be just fine."*

⁵¹ Well, the man headed back home just like Jesus done said. He rode all night! Early the next mornin', he saw his servants was a-runnin' to meet him. They were a-hollerin', "Your boy lives! Yes-sir-ee, he's doin' just fine!"

⁵² He figured to ask them just when did his boy start gettin' better? "Yesterday afternoon 'round one o'clock. All of a sudden the fever just up and left him!"

⁵³ It was just like he figured. The fever left his boy at the very time that Jesus said, *"Your boy's doin' fine."* And because of that he believed in Jesus and so did everybody else in his outfit.

⁵⁴ This miracle was reckoned as the second sign that Jesus did after He had come out of Judea and into Galilee.

Thinkin' Questions

1. Do you believe Jesus still performs miracles today? If yes, do you have a personal experience with miracles to share?

2. Does a strong faith make a miracle more likely?____ Or not?____ Explain your thoughts. **Read Matthew 9:22; Mark 10:51-52; Luke 17:11-19 & Mark 2:3-5.**

3. What about unanswered prayers for a miracle? Does that mean our faith doesn't measure up? Or that God doesn't care for us as much as someone else? **See Romans 5:1-8 & Romans 8:18, 25, 37-39 and 2 Corinthians 12:7-10.**

4. In the story above, how did the government man show that he had faith in Jesus? **Read also Matthew 15:22-28.** Is it enough to believe Jesus can heal?

5. Is it wrong to have faith based in part on miracles? Explain. **Refer to Luke 10:23-24 and John 20:29-31.**

Chapter Five

Healin' Beside a Pond

¹ Now it was time to move on to Jerusalem; Jesus had work to do, so He rode on up the trail.

² It just so happened that along the sheep gate in Jerusalem was a fancy pool of water. It had a bunch of porches all around it.

³ There were lots of sick folks gathered all around there with all kinds of sicknesses; some of 'em was blind, some lame, some a-witherin' away about to die. They were waitin' for the water to start stirrin'.

⁴ Ya see it was believed in those days that one of God's angels came down and stirred up that particular pond once in awhile. Whoever was first to get into that water after it was stirred up would be healed of his ailments.

⁵ There was one particular fella who had been comin' there just about all his life, near thirty-eight years.

⁶ When Jesus saw him restin' there, He knew every single day the fella had suffered. I 'xpect Jesus called him by name and He just asked him, "*Do you want to be well?*"

Chapter 5 ℰℂℛ Just Thinkin

Westward bound, a mother cried out desperately to God for rain when her little son in their covered wagon had come down with a fever and there was no water. Soon a small cloud began to form overhead. God hears our prayers and only He can meet the deepest needs of our lives. He heals in many ways. The man at the pool of Bethesda had waited years, hoping for a cure. He was cured of his ailment, not by the churning of the waters of Bethesda, but only when Jesus came and met his desperate need with His healing presence.

ℰℂℛ

⁷ The sick man answered, "Mister, I don't have a pardner or a side kick to help me to the water. When the water starts movin', well Sir, it takes me so long to get there, somebody else done already gets there first, but I keep comin' here. I ain't givin' up yet."

⁸ Jesus replied to the man, "*Come on, pardner, get on up. Get your bedroll there and let's walk outta here.*"

Thinkin' Questions

1. Why do you think Jesus asked the man if he wanted to get well? **Read verse 6.** He had been coming for 38 years. Wasn't it obvious? Look at another example: **Matthew 20:29-34.**

2. After the command of Jesus to "get up", the man's next move will reveal his faith and belief . . . or not. When you receive a command from God through His word, (the Bible), how does your response reveal faith and belief? Or not?

⁹ And just like that, the man was on his feet like there was nothin' wrong with him. Yep, and he rolled up his bed and began to stroll on out of there. It was the Sabbath day, by the way.

¹⁰ And then, would ya believe it, some of them religious know-it-alls started makin a ruckus. They were a-houndin' the man and sayin', "It's the Sabbath and you ain't supposed to be carryin' your bedroll like that!"

¹¹ They was a-givin' this fella some serious trouble, so he started tellin' 'em, "There was this One who healed me and told me to pick up my bed and walk. Who was I to argue?"

¹² "Alright then," they said, "Where is this Man now? Where's the One ya say told ya to do it?"

¹³ But the plain truth is the man didn't know for sure who Jesus was or where He had gone, because Jesus had done slipped away in the big crowd of folks in that place.

Thinkin' Questions

1. Is there such a thing as being over-religious? Explain:

2. Do you think Jesus wants us to be religious?

3. According to the Bible, what is the place of religion in our relationship with Jesus Christ? **Read Matthew 23:23-24; 2 Corinthians 3:1-6; Ephesians 2:8-10 and James 1:26-27.**

4. Why do you think Jesus left the man to answer for himself with the Jews that day?

¹⁴ Later, Jesus sure 'nough found the man in the temple. Reckon He wanted to finish His conversation with him. He told the man, "Now *that you are well, don't sin anymore so that nothin' worse happens to ya.*"

¹⁵ Then the man went and told those religious what-nots, the ones who was causin' trouble for him, "It was Jesus who done made me well."

¹⁶ So the Jews went to give Jesus a powerful hard time for what they figured was "breakin' the Sabbath." Ain't right, is it?

Thinkin' Questions

1. Why do you think Jesus went back to find the man He healed at the pool? **See Matthew 10:32-33.**

2. What does this say to you about Jesus' personal dealings with us?

3. What do you think He meant when He said, *"so that nothing worse happens to you?"* **Read Luke 12:4-7.**

[17] Well, Jesus had no problem speakin' right up to those dudes. He told 'em, *"My Father has been workin' right up 'til now and I Myself am workin' too."*

[18] Those fellas about choked on that statement alright. They was all the more determined after that to find a way to get rid of Jesus. They already wanted to kill Him for breakin' their Sabbath laws, and now He had just said that God was His very own Father and was a-makin' Himself out to be on level ground with God.

[19] Jesus just kept talkin'. He said, *"I'm tellin' y'all the truth. The Son can't do anything by Himself. It's gotta be somethin' He sees His Father doin', then He can join in with the Father's work and do just like Him."*

[20] *"Ya see, the Father loves His Son and shows Him everything He's a-doin'. And thrown in with that, the Father will show Him even bigger things to do that will plumb knock your boots off!"*

> Chapter 5   Just Thinkin
> The closest I ever felt to my father was the summer he and I spent working together building a barn and corral. From start to finish; from foundation to the roof we worked side by side. By listening to him and following his example I not only learned how to saw, nail and read a blueprint but I also learned a lot about my dad. Jesus had much to say about His Father. He talked about His closeness to Him. He talked to His Father often and made it clear that He could do nothing by Himself.

[21] *"I'm tellin' ya, just like the Father raises the dead and gives life back to them, the Son can give life to anyone He wants to."*

Thinkin' Questions

1. According to Jesus' own words in **verse 19** how did He know on a daily basis what God wanted Him to do according to the Father's will? **Read John 14:9-10.**

2. How did Jesus know what the Father was up to? **Mark 1:35-39; Luke 4:42-44; Luke 6:12.**

3. What did Jesus mean *"the Son can do _nothing_ by Himself"*? **Read John 7:16; John 8:28; John 12:49 and John 17:8.**

²²⁻²³ "I want y'all to understand; the Father has given Me the whole job of judgin' the world in days to come. He wants y'all to think of Me and treat Me just like you're supposed to treat Him. Folks who refuse to honor Me; they disrespect the Father who sent Me in the first place.

²⁴ I surely want everybody to know that any fella or gal who listens to what I've got to say and believes in the One who sent Me has life that is everlastin', and he or she will never go through the judgment. No-sir-ee, they have already passed from death to life forever.

²⁵ And let Me tell ya somethin' else; already the dead are a-hearin' the voice of the Son of God; and those who hear Me will live.

²⁶ Ya see, the Father is the Giver of life, yes-sir-ee, and He has given that same power to the Son so He can also give life from Himself."

²⁷ Jesus went on sayin', "And 'sides that, He gave His Son the right to judge 'cause He is the Son of Man and duly qualified.

²⁸⁻²⁹ So don't get all hankered up when one day all the folks who are dead and buried hear His voice and come walkin' right out of their graves; --the ones who have done the right thing will be raised up to life, and those who have done evil will be raised up for damnation.

³⁰ Ya see, I don't do anything of My own self. I judge based on what I hear the Father sayin' to Me; and My judgment is right. It can't be anything else because I only look to do the perfect will of the Father who sent Me."

Thinkin' Questions

1. **Read John 12:47-50.** How does it fit with Jesus' words here in **chapter 5:27-30**?

2. What makes a person worthy to by-pass *"the judgment"* described in **Revelation 20:11-15?**

3. If we, as believers do not face judgment, how are we accountable for the way we live our lives? **See Romans 14:10-12; 2 Corinthians 5:9-10 and 1 John 2:1-2.**

4. Jesus is the Conqueror of death and Giver of life, our Judge, and our Savior. Do you personally know Jesus Christ as the One who will walk you past the judgment and into eternity? Write down your thoughts.

³¹ *"If it was just Me testifyin' about My own self, I wouldn't be expectin' anybody just to take My word for it.*

³² *There is another who vouches for Me and I don't doubt His word. It's a sure thing that what He says about Me is true.*

³³ *Some of you cowpokes have sent to John the Baptist askin' him what the truth is about Me.*

³⁴ *But I'm a-tellin' ya, the words I speak are not from any man, no-sir-ee! But I am a-tellin' y'all how it really is, so you can get yourselves right with God Almighty.*

³⁵ *Now, ol' John, he was the best light y'all had for a spell. He was burnin' bright and shinin' for all to see. Most folks found that to be a mighty good thing.*

³⁶ *But I'm tellin' ya, John was just gettin' y'all ready for somethin' else. Ya see, I've come along now bringin' y'all much more than John did 'cause the work that the Father gave Me to get done; well even the work itself testifies to Who I Am and that the Father Himself done sent Me.*

³⁷ *That being said, He also agrees and testifies about Me. But y'all have never heard His voice and neither have you seen Him.*

³⁸ *Y'all don't have His word in your heart. I know 'cause you don't believe Me, the very One He sent."*

Thinkin' Questions

1. In **verses 36 & 37** above, what and who testifies about who Jesus is:

2. Do we have another One whose word is sure to testify of Jesus Christ today? **Read John 14:25-26; John 15:26-27; 1 John 5:6-8; John 16:12-15; Acts 5:32 and Romans 8:16.** List some of His names:

3. What is the *"somethin' else"* that Jesus spoke of in **verse 36**? **See Luke 4:14-21; Mark 8:31; 1 Corinthians 15:1-4.**

³⁹ *"Y'all search through the Scriptures lookin' for everlastin' life when all the while it's the Scriptures that are a-testifyin' about Me.*

⁴⁰ *But y'all have done refused to see it, and so you still won't come to Me and live.*

⁴¹⁻⁴² *Anyway, it is not from men that I get glory. Ya see, I know you; I mean I really know each of ya. I can see that y'all don't have the love of God in yourselves."*

⁴³ *Jesus wasn't through yet. He went on sayin', "I have come here in My Father's good name and y'all don't accept Me; but if someone else comes in his own name, I reckon you swallow what he has to say if it suits ya.*

⁴⁴ *How is it that y'all give and receive glory all around with each other, but you shy away from the glory that has come from only God Himself?*

⁴⁵ *I'm not accusin' anybody. I don't have to 'cause y'all have already been accused by Moses, the one you're hopin' will save you.*

⁴⁶ *But the thing is if you really believed Moses, you'd believe Me, too. Ya see Moses wrote about Me, yes-sir-ee.*

⁴⁷ *But if you don't believe his writings, then you're not likely to believe My words."*

Thinkin' Questions

1. In addition to the Father, the Son, the Holy Spirit, the works of Jesus, and John the Baptist, what else also testifies of Jesus Christ? **Read Verse 39.**

2. Who recorded the Scriptures that religious leaders in Jesus' day would be searching? **See Verse 46.**

3. Read other passages that confirm the identity of Jesus. **Luke 4:17-21; Matthew 2:22-23; Matthew 26:55-56; Luke 18:31; Luke 24:25-27 & 44-49; John 1:45 and Acts 3:18.**

4. According to the prophecy of the Scriptures, what is the next big event concerning Jesus Christ? **Read 1 Thessalonians 4:15-18.**

Chapter Six

The Bread of Life

¹ After a spell, Jesus made His way along the trail on over to the other side of the Sea of Galilee, or as some call it, Tiberias.

² A big lot of folks followed after Him because they had seen His miracles and had done learned that He could make sick people well.

³ Jesus went on up the hill a ways to sit a spell with His pardners.

⁴ Now the biggest feast day of the year was not far off, that is the Passover.

⁵ Jesus hardly sat down 'til He looked up and saw a huge herd of folks a-comin' for more teachin' and healin'. He tested His pardner Philip by askin' him, *"Where do you reckon we'll buy bread to feed all these people who are a-comin'?"*

⁶ Ya know He done already knew what He was fixin' to do, but He asked anyway.

⁷ Philip scratched his head, "Not even eight months of wranglin' cattle would give us enough dough to buy 'em all a mouthful."

⁸ Then one of the other pardners, ol' Andrew, Peter's brother, he spoke up,

⁹ "All we got is this little cowboy here that's got five biscuits and a couple of little perch packed for his lunch. Reckon what good is that for so many folks that need to eat?"

Thinkin' Questions

1. Notice Jesus questioning Philip and the other disciples in **verse 5**. Why does God ask us questions that He already knows the answer to? **Refer to: Genesis 3:9 & 13; Genesis 4:9-10; Luke 18:41 and Luke 24:17-19.**

2. What does getting us to think for ourselves have to do with our faith? **Look at Luke 8:25; Matthew 9:21-22; Matthew 15:24-28 and Romans 10:13-14 & 17.**

3. What does Jesus want us to be aware of regarding our abilities versus His power? **See John 15:5 and Isaiah 40:28-31.**

[10] When Jesus heard that He said, *"Have the folks all sit down on the big grassy place yonder."* And when they all got sat down there was about five thousand men, not countin' the women and young'uns! Now that's a big herd!

[11] Jesus gave thanks for the biscuits and they started passin' them around. Then He did the same with the fish 'til every single one had plenty.

[12] When everyone was plumb full and done eatin', Jesus said to His pardners, *"Go and gather up all the leftovers so that nothin' is wasted."*

[13] So the pardners took their saddle bags or knapsacks --whatever they had; and they filled up twelve bags of biscuits and fish for tomorrow's supper.

[14] All them folks was rightly amazed when they saw this miracle, yes-sir-ee. They declared right then, *"This here is surely the Prophet we've been a-hearin' about who's supposed to come into the world!"*

[15] Jesus knew what they were thinkin'. He reckoned they were about to grab hold of Him right then and there to make Him King. So He slipped away by Hisself and went on up the hill.

Chapter 6   Just Thinkin

One ol' cowboy said two miracles were done that day when Jesus fed the 5000. One was that a boy had gone that long without eating his lunch and the other was the feeding of that large multitude of people with a boy's meager portion. But what a miracle it was when Jesus took that young lad's lunch that consisted of a handful of biscuits and a couple of small fish and with His blessings fed a multitude of thousands. By this miracle we can know the way it is when Jesus blesses something. He can take that which is small and make it big. He can take the offering of our service and use it to the greater good for His Kingdom. Never underestimate what God can do with what little we hand to Him in faith.

Thinkin' Questions

1. Ever wished you could perform a miracle like this when unexpected company shows up at your house at mealtime? Jesus performs a creative miracle for food in the above passage. Yet, when He was fasting in the wilderness He refused to use this miraculous power. **Read Matthew 4:1-4.** How is this different?

2. Jesus could have become King when He walked this earth and righted all the wrongs of His day. For instance, He could have wiped out human disease. Why didn't He take this opportunity? **Read John 18:33-37.**

3. What does prophecy reveal to us about Jesus one day ruling as King of Kings and Lord of Lords. **Read Revelation 19:11-16 & 21:1-4.**

[16] When it started gettin' dark, His pardners all went on back down to the seashore.

[17] After gettin' the boat all ready to set sail, it was about to get real dark; and they had to get goin' off across to Capernaum to spend the night, even though Jesus hadn't caught up yet.

[18] Sure 'nough, a big windstorm came up and the waves began to get powerful rough.

[19] Jesus' pardners rowed and rowed, but they had only made a few miles, not even halfway across fightin' that wind. All of a sudden, the lightnin' flashed and they saw Jesus walkin' on the water comin' to 'em. They were mighty scared, sure 'nough.

[20] But Jesus hollered out to them, *"Howdy! Don't be scared! It's Me!"*

[21] They gladly welcomed Him aboard, n' just like that, the boat was comin' ashore at the place where they were aimin' to go in the first place. Whew!

[22] When morning came, the crowd that were back on the other side saw that the only boat that had gone across the way was the pardners' boat. One thing those folks knew for sure; Jesus had not gone out in that boat with His buddies.

[23-24] Then some other boats showed up from Tiberias. They put in 'bout where Jesus had gave thanks and fed that whole crowd. Some folks loaded up in the Tiberias boats for a ride across after they figured Jesus' pardners were long gone. Word had spread and everybody was a-lookin' for Jesus.

[25] They sure were surprised when they made it across the sea and there was Jesus, (and He was all rested up, too). "Teacher," they said, "How did you get here?"

[26] Jesus told 'em straight like always, *"I know why y'all are lookin' for Me. It is not because by the signs, you know who I am. But it's because you ate and got your bellies full, and y'all want some more bread."*

Thinkin' Question

1. It is a tragedy now as it was then for folks to see Jesus only as a miracle worker or healer; only a provider for their needs or a fix for their problems. Others see Him as a great teacher without truly knowing Him as Christ, Messiah, Savior and Redeemer. What can we do as believers to help prevent the misidentification of Jesus today?

²⁷ Jesus went on to tell the folks, *"Don't just be workin' for food to fill your stomachs. That will not last. But the food that the Son of Man gives you, now that will fill your heart and last forever through the hereafter. For ya see, God the Father has already set His mark of approval on the Son of Man."*

²⁸⁻²⁹ *"Well then,"* they said. *"What do we do, so we can work the works of God?"* Jesus told 'em plain, *"Here is the work of God: Believe in the One that He sent."*

Thinkin' Questions

1. Jesus is using the illustration of food in **verse 27** to teach a spiritual principle. What food is Jesus referring to that will last for eternity? **Read Matthew 6:25; John 4:32-34; 1 Corinthians 3:1-2 and Hebrews 5:12-14.**

2. In the Old Testament, how important is it to God that we believe Him? Refer to **Numbers 14:11-12; Numbers 20:12 Psalms 106:24-27 and Isaiah 43:10-11.**

3. It seems no matter how much grace is offered, our nature is to want to justify ourselves with God by good works. What does it mean to simply *"believe"*? What are the results?

    Mark 1:15-17--verse 15 "_____ and believe"; --verse 17 "_____ Me"
    Mark 5:36 "Do not _____, _____ believe"
    Mark 9:23 "all things _____ _____ for one who _____."
    John 3:36 "Whoever believes in the Son has _____."
    Acts 10:43 "everyone who believes in Him receives _____."
    Hebrews 11:6 "whoever would draw near to God must _____".
    1 John 5:5 "Who is it that overcomes…..? the one who _____ that Jesus is the Son of God.

4. Are works involved in salvation in any way? **Read Romans 3:23-24 & 27-28; also Ephesians 2:8-10.**

5. What kind of impact could pure and simple belief in Jesus have on our lives and on our world? Write down your thoughts.

³⁰ They said to Jesus, "So You say . . . well, then show us a sign that we can take Your word for it. We need to see somethin' that would make us believe."

³¹ "Our ancestors ate that manna don't ya know, out there in the wilderness. The Good Book says, 'Moses done gave them bread out of heaven to eat.'"

³² Jesus kept on trying to get through to these folks. He explained further, *The truth is, it wasn't Moses who gave the bread out of heaven, but My Father. He also is the One givin' y'all the true bread out of heaven.*

³³ *Ya see, the bread of God is what comes on down out of heaven and gives life to the world.*

³⁴ So they rightly spoke up, "Lord! That's the bread we want, give that to us from here on out."

Thinkin' Questions

1. Do you think Jesus and these He is speaking with are talking about the same type of *"bread"*?

Chapter 6   Just Thinkin

A family was making their way out west by covered wagon when they were suddenly surrounded by Indians. With gestures and broken English they made the woman understand that they wanted her to make them a pan of biscuits. She did so and after eating the hot buttered biscuits the little band of Indians rode away never to be seen again. That day, the Indians hunger was temporarily satisfied with bread prepared by a pioneer woman. There is a greater hunger than physical; and that is a spiritual hunger. Only Jesus can satisfy that emptiness. "Then Jesus just came right out and told 'em, *I am the Bread of Life. He who comes to Me will not hunger, and he who believes in Me will never thirst"* (John 6:35).

2. What are the similarities between our relationship with Jesus and the *"manna"* in the wilderness? **Read Exodus 16:14-21; Deuteronomy 8:3; Luke 9:23; Psalm 68:19; Matthew 6:11.**

3. Personally speaking, what does the *"True Bread out of Heaven"* mean for you in your everyday life?

[35] Then Jesus just came right out and told 'em, *"I am the Bread of Life. He who comes to Me will not hunger, and he who believes in Me will never thirst.*

[36] *But even though I have told y'all and you have seen Me, y'all just don't believe.*

[37-38] *It's like this, all the folks that My Pa gives to Me will come to Me; and not a one of them will be turned away or tossed out. I have come down from heaven, not to do My own will, but to do the will of the One who sent Me.*

[39] *This is what the One who sent Me is set on: that of everyone and everything He has given Me, I lose nary a one, but I will raise 'em all up on the last day.*

[40] *Here is a sure thing, yes-sir-ee. You can bet your life on this: Everyone who sees the Son and believes in Him will live forever, and I Myself will raise him up on the last day."*

Thinkin' Questions

1. In **verse 35,** Jesus tells us He is the *Bread of Life* represented by the manna in the wilderness. He also reveals He will continually quench the thirst of our souls as well. What Old Testament icon is Jesus referring to here? **Read Exodus 17:6; Psalm 105:41; Isaiah 48:21; Also read John 7:37-39. Review John 4:13-14.**

2. In **verses 36-40,** Jesus reminds us that not everyone will believe in Him. When He walked this earth many people saw and heard Him and witnessed His miracles. Still there were those who rejected Him. However, for those who accept Him what is His promise? **Read John 17:12; John 10:28-29; Romans 8:35-39; 2 Corinthians 1:21-22; Ephesians 1:13-14 and Ephesians 4:30-32.**

3. Jesus turned the subject to the last day of the world as we know it in **verse 40.** What hope do we, as believers have on that day? **See verse 40** "I Myself will _____ _____ _____ "

4. Read the following verses in your Bible that assure us of our resurrection:

Historical evidence:	**Biblical Promise:**
John 11:38-44	John 5:28-29; John 11:25
Matthew 27:50-53	1 Thessalonians 4:15-18
Mark 5:35-42	Romans 6:5
Luke 7:12-15	1 Corinthians 15:20-23
Mark 16:2-7,9,12,14	Revelation 20:6

⁴¹ But don't ya know, the religious Jews done got all offended and commenced grumblin' against Him because He said He was the bread that came down out of heaven.

⁴² Now they was just sayin', "Ain't this Jesus the son of Joseph, whose ma and pa we know? Who does He think He is a-sayin', 'I have come down out of heaven?'"

⁴³ Jesus knew what they were sayin'. He told 'em, "You fellas be careful. Don't be bad-mouthin' Me amongst yourselves.

⁴⁴ "Y'all might want to pray for yourselves because not a single soul can come to Me unless the Father who sent Me draws him; and they are the ones I will surely raise up on the last day."

Thinkin' Questions

1. In **verses 41 & 42**, the Jews are having difficulty fitting Jesus into their religious beliefs. What is causing them to take offense and stumble over the very One who can bring salvation? **Read Isaiah 8:14; Romans 9:30-33 and 1 Peter 2:6-8.**

2. Is Jesus still a "stumbling block" or even a "Rock of offense" to some people today? Why?

3. In **verse 44**, Jesus tells these who are so embedded in their religion that no one can come to God on their own. How does God work in our lives to draw us to Himself? **Read Jeremiah 31:3 and Hosea 11:3-4** from the Old Testament.

4. What or Who makes it possible for us to come to God? **See John 6:65.**

5. Is there anything that we can do to get close to God? **Look at James 4:6-10.**

⁴⁵ *The prophets wrote it down in the Word of God, 'And they shall all be taught of God.' Ya see everybody who has heard and learned from the Father comes to Me.*

⁴⁶ *Not that anyone has laid eyes on the Father, 'cept the One who is from God; He has seen the Father.*

⁴⁷ *I'm shootin' straight with y'all. Every person who believes in Me has everlastin' life.*

⁴⁸ *I am the Bread of Life.*

⁴⁹ *Your relatives that came along before you ate the bread in the wilderness and they died.*

⁵⁰ *This is the bread that comes down out of heaven. Anyone can eat of it and not die.*

⁵¹ *I am the Living Bread that came down out of heaven; if anyone eats this bread, he or she is gonna live forever; and the bread that I am a-givin' is My own flesh, so the whole world can have the forever kind of life."*

⁵² Now that about put the Jews over the edge. They just didn't get it. They were arguin'. Some were thinkin' it, and some were sayin', "How can this cowboy stand there and say He is gonna give His flesh for us to eat?"

Thinkin' Questions

1. In **verse 45**, Jesus says that the truth of God is not discovered, but actually revealed by God the Father. To what kind of heart does God reveal Himself? **Read 1 Corinthians 2:9-10 & 14-16; Galatians 1:11-12 & 15-16a.**

2. In **verse 47**, what does Jesus say is already ours when we open our hearts to receive Him?

3. In **Jeremiah 31:31-34**, the prophet describes the new covenant. From what you have learned so far, describe how it differs from the old beliefs regarding our relationship to God and the Law?

Chapter Six – The Bread of Life

⁵³ Jesus told 'em straight, but he was speakin' to 'em about their souls, not their stomachs, *"I'm tellin' you fellas, unless you receive Me into your souls just like you would eat and drink food into your bodies; well then, you just ain't got life in yourselves. Spiritually speakin' you're good as dead.*

⁵⁴⁻⁵⁵ *But if anyone partakes of Me, on account I have come as flesh and blood, they will live on after this life and I will raise him or her up from the grave on the last day. For ya see, believin' in My flesh is true food and believin' in My blood is true drink for any cowboy or cowgirl who wants to have the kind of life that lasts forever.*

⁵⁶ *The folks that make Messiah a part of themselves by taking Him fully into their very soul will abide in Him forever and I will abide forever in each and every one of them.*

⁵⁷ *Ya see, I live by the power of My Father who sent Me, and in the same way, those who partake of Me shall live because of Me.*

⁵⁸ *It's like I told ya, I am the True Bread which came down from heaven, not like the bread your forefathers done ate and died, no-sir-ee. But if you eat this Bread, you will live forever."*

⁵⁹ Now Jesus done said all this in the meetin' place in Capernaum.

⁶⁰ And after He said these things, a bunch of His pardners said, "Them are some mighty thorny words to listen to."

⁶¹ Jesus knew His pardners was havin' a hard time with what He'd been sayin' so He asked 'em outright, *"Is this trippin' y'all up?"*

⁶² *"If y'all are havin' trouble with this, what are ya gonna do when you see Me, the Son of Man, goin' back up to heaven where I was before?"*

⁶³ *Ya see fellas, only the Holy Spirit gives everlastin' life; your flesh can't get that for ya. These things I've been a-sayin' to y'all are spirit. There's life in these words of Mine for sure.*

⁶⁴ *But some of y'all here don't believe Me."* The truth is, Jesus already knew who they were; that is, them who would not believe. And He knew the one who was gonna turn against Him, too.

⁶⁵ So then He said, *"This is why I've been tellin' y'all that no one can truly come to Me unless the Father Himself allows it."*

⁶⁶ Just then, a bunch of folks who had been followin' Jesus around real excited like, well they jumped on their horses and just rode away. I guess they done heard all they wanted to hear.

⁶⁷ Jesus turned then to His twelve pardners still standin' there, *"Y'all gonna up and ride off too?"* He asked.

[68] Well, ol' Peter ya know, he spoke up, "No-sir-ee, I reckon we'll stay on, Boss. Ain't nowhere else to go since You've got them words of everlastin' life You've been a-tellin' us about. Where else would we go off to?

[69] On account I reckon all of us have 'bout figured it out that You are the Holy One of God. Yes-sir-ee, we believe it."

[70] Then Jesus looked 'em square in the eyes and said, *"Didn't I Myself choose all twelve of you? Yet one of you is a devil."*

[71] Now that took 'em by surprise. They didn't know it, but Jesus was talkin' about Judas Iscariot. He knew that ol' Judas couldn't help himself. In days ahead he would be the one that would put a knife right in Jesus' back.

Ponder This:

In the last 18 verses of our study of Chapter Six, Jesus explains Himself again by using word pictures and illustrations from the Old Testament of which Jews were familiar. However, speaking of spiritual things often sounds foolish to those whose hearts and minds are closed to The Holy Spirit of God. Jesus assured the disciples that it was no accident they were with Him. It was by the will of the Father He had chosen them. Indeed we are chosen in Christ before the foundation of the world. He knows our hearts. It is no accident you are participating in Bible study at this very time. The Lord Jesus Christ is indeed working in your life.

Reflection: In what ways has God revealed Himself to you personally through your own life experiences? Describe how your faith has been strengthened.

Chapter Seven

Causin' a Ruckus

¹ Jesus moved on up the trail stayin' in the saddle around Galilee and steerin' plumb away from Judea down the road. He knew there was a bushwhack waitin' for Him around those parts.

²⁻³ Now there was a big ol' Jewish shindig comin' up called the "Feast of Booths". They had it every year along about the same time. So His brothers said to Him, "Why don't Ya just go on down there so all them pardners of Yours in Jerusalem can see the things folks around here claim to have seen.

⁴ It ain't no good to try to be a-doin' somethin' when You're hidin' out. If You want the whole world to know about Ya like Ya say, go ahead and show Your hand!"

⁵ Truth is Jesus' brothers were chidin' Him 'cause they didn't believe in Him yet.

⁶ Jesus told 'em flat out, "It isn't time yet for Me to show My hand, but your time to believe is always right here and now.

⁷ The world does not hate you fellas yet, but I reckon I know the condition of things now and I speak up about it, so it surely does hate Me. Ya see, the ways of the world are just plain evil.

⁸⁻⁹ So y'all git yourselves on down to that feast. I know folks are expectin' Me to show up with y'all, but it's not the right time for that yet." So Jesus stayed behind.

Chapter 7 — Just Thinkin

The Feast of Tabernacles celebrated each year looks back to Israel's journey in the wilderness. For a week each year the Jews live in lean-tos or tents made of branches to remind them of God's continual watch care over the nation for forty years (Leviticus 23:33-44). It is a festive time for the people. Huge candlesticks illumine the Temple to remind folks of God's guiding pillar of fire. Water is carried from the Pool of Siloam each day to remind them of God's provision of water in the barren wilderness. Jesus is still the provision for our dry barren lives today as He was then. As He cried out to the Jews that day, He still cries out to us: *"If any one of y'all is thirsty, let him come to Me and drink! Any fellow or gal that believes in Me . . . will come to have rivers of living water gushin' forth from deep inside."* John 7:37-38

Thinkin' Questions

1. The *"feast of booths"* is still practiced today by devout Jews. What is the significance of this observance? **Read Leviticus 23:39-43.**

2. What do you think Jesus' brothers were up to in **verses 3 & 4**?

3. Jesus revealed Divine insight in **verses 6-9. What was it**?

¹⁰ Now Jesus gave His brothers plenty of time to get down to the feast, and then He saddled up and headed out for the feast Himself. He figured He would slip in kinda quiet like.

¹¹ Ya see, the religious big shots who had give Jesus so much trouble, they was lookin' for Him and askin' all around, "Where is He?"

¹² The crowd was plumb up in arms about Jesus. A bunch of 'em were sayin', "He's a Man you can ride the river with!" Others were sayin', "No way, He's gone off the trail we've been on since way back."

¹³ But nobody was speakin' up out in the open in favor of Jesus, 'cause folks were a-feared of the trouble that might come their way from those Jewish religious honchos.

¹⁴ But after the feast done got underway Jesus showed up at the temple. It weren't long 'til He just started in teachin'.

¹⁵ Then the Jewish folk were dumbfounded saying, "He has no formal learnin' so how can He know so much?"

¹⁶⁻¹⁷ Jesus spoke right up to 'em like always, *"My teachin' is not Mine, but it comes from the One who done sent Me. And if there is any fella or gal who is agreeable to do His will, then I reckon they will know, sure as fire, whether this teachin' is from God or if I speak for Myself."*

Thinkin' Questions

1. We know that Jesus does not lie or deceive. **(Hebrews 4:15; 1 Peter 2:22)** We also know that Jesus is not influenced by peer or family pressure. What do you think happened in **verse 10** in order for Jesus to go to the feast after declining in **verses 8-9?** What is going on here? **Read John 5:19-20; John 6:38; John 8:28-29.** Write down your thoughts.

2. The authority of Jesus, His actions and the timing of those actions are directed by
_____. **(John 5:19)**

¹⁸ "The fella that speaks for his own self is lookin' for his own glory; but He who is lookin' for the glory of the One who sent Him, He is the true One, and there's no blame or wrong in Him.

¹⁹ Yer' old grandpappy, Moses, gave you the Law, didn't he? And yet not one of y'all carries out the Law. Why in thunder then are you hankerin' to kill Me?"

²⁰ Some folks in the crowd who was hearin' Jesus shouted, "You're talkin' crazy now! You have a demon! Who's lookin' to kill You?"

²¹ Jesus spoke up then, "I do a good thing and y'all are amazed, but some of you don't like it.

²² Ol' Moses gave you circumcision as a mark passed down from his father Abraham. And y'all circumcise on the Sabbath day, right?

²³ Now, if a man can be circumcised on the Sabbath, how come y'all get all up in arms at Me 'cause I make a maimed cowboy well on the Sabbath?"

²⁴ Jesus told 'em straight, "Y'all are hung up on how stuff looks from the outside. You better judge by what God says is right in your heart."

²⁵ But some of these folks were thinkin', "This sure 'nough might be the Man that they are lookin' to kill."

Thinkin' Questions

1. What *"good thing"* in **verses 21-23** might Jesus be referring to that He did on the Sabbath? **Read John 5:1-9, 16-17.**

2. Why were the religious leaders seeking to kill Jesus? **Read John 5:18.**

3. No one likes to be misjudged and misunderstood, including Jesus. Neither did He like seeing the Old Testament Law misused and misinterpreted. In your own words, what is Jesus trying to say in **verses 23 & 24?**

²⁶ Others were a-sayin', "Well, I don't know, here He is talkin' out in the open and they ain't sayin' nothin' to Him. Them religious rulers don't know if He is the Christ or not, do they?

²⁷ Well we know whereabouts this man is from. But when Christ comes, will anybody rightly know where He comes from?"

²⁸ With that kind of talk goin' on, Jesus spoke mighty powerful, *"Y'all know Me and you know where I came from. I've told y'all that My coming was not of Myself, but the One who sent Me. He is true, but y'all don't know Him."*

²⁹ Jesus told 'em flat out, *"I know Him, 'cause I am from Him, and He sent Me."*

³⁰ Knowin' He was speakin' of God the Father, some of the crowd got plenty riled up and proceeded to try to take Him out; but nobody could put their hands on Him because the time for that hadn't come yet, no-sir-ee!

³¹ But a right smart number of the folks there that day did believe in Jesus. They were tryin' to reason with the others quiet-like sayin, "When the Christ comes, do you suppose He will do more miracles than this Man's done?"

³² The Pharisees heard what was bein' said. They figured they better put a stop to it, so they got up a posse to nab Jesus." (But they didn't get Him, not yet).

Thinkin' Questions

1. Jesus has tried to clearly identify Himself. People were speculating as to whether or not He is indeed Christ, the Messiah. What were they basing their judgment on in **verse 27**? **Read 1 Corinthians 1:18-25.**

2. **Verse 31** reminds us that amidst the unbelief, rejection and plans to kill Jesus, there were those who were believing in Him. Their voice of reason seemed small, but hearts were being healed and the Kingdom of Christ was growing. Why do we continue to proclaim the Gospel in a world that seems so anti-Christian these days? **Look at John 1:9-13 and Acts 17:32-34.**

³³ Then Jesus said, *"I'm gonna be with y'all for a little while longer, then I'm going back to the One who sent Me.*

³⁴ *When I ride out, y'all can't follow to where I'm goin'. Y'all will be a-lookin' out for Me but you won't find Me."*

³⁵ The Jews all began sayin' amongst themselves, "Now where do you reckon He figures on goin' that we can't find Him? Ya don't suppose He's intendin' to go to them that got scattered, and start teachin' amongst the Greeks, do ya?"

³⁶ *"Just what in thunder does He mean sayin', 'Y'all are gonna be looking for Me, but you won't find Me 'cause where I am y'all can't come?'"*

Thinkin' Questions

1. What is Jesus is trying to tell His followers in **verses 33 & 34?**

2. What do we know about where Jesus is going? **Read John 8:21 & 23-24; John 13:33 & 36; also John 14:1-6 & 28.**

[37] When the last and biggest day of the feast came around Jesus spoke out to the crowd so they all could hear Him, yes-sir-ee! He hollered out, *"If any one of y'all is thirsty, let him come to Me and drink!*

[38] *Any fellow or gal that believes in Me like the Good Book says, will come to have rivers of living water gushin' forth from deep inside."*

[39] Now Jesus, sure 'nough, was a-speakin' about the Holy Spirit who would later come to reside in each one who believed. But first, Jesus had to be glorified through His death on the cross and His resurrection, don't ya see.

[40] Some of the folks who done heard these words of Jesus said, "You can bet your boots, this is the Prophet!"

Thinkin' Questions

1. Jesus told the woman at the well in **John 4:13-14** about *"living water"*. Here once again Jesus introduces the concept of the indwelling Holy Spirit of God in a person's life. Jesus chose the illustration of *Living Water* to describe the Holy Spirit. Review how the Holy Spirit is like water? **Read Matthew 5:6; John 6:35; Revelation 21:6 and Revelation 22:17.**

2. Name three things described as *"flowing"* or *"proceeding"* directly from God to us through Jesus Christ based on the following verses.

   His _____ **Matthew 4:4**

   His _____ **John 15:26**

   His _____ **Luke 6:17-19; Luke 8:45-46**

3. Can you name some other things that are described as *"given"* or *"poured out"* that we receive from God through Jesus Christ? **Here are a few: Luke 24:49; Romans 5:5; Ephesians 4:7-8; 1 John 5:11; Revelation 22:1.**

[41] Others said, "This is the Christ!" But then some of those religious troublemakers sneered sayin', "Surely I never heard nothin' 'bout the Christ comin' from Galilee, did you?"

[42] They went on, "Don't the Good Book say that the Christ comes from Bethlehem, from the line of David?"

[43] Folks began takin' sides and a heated argument rose up amongst the crowd.

[44] Now that posse that was sent out were of a mind to get their hands on Jesus, but no one was able to lay a finger on Him, no-sir-ee.

[45] So the posse came back to them hot-shot Pharisees and religious chiefs without Jesus as their prisoner. Those religious fellas wanted to know, "Why didn't you get Jesus and bring Him here like we told you?"

[46] But the men replied, "Never has there been a man who speaks the way this Fella does."

[47] The Pharisees sputtered out, "Y'all ain't fallin' for Him are you?"

Thinkin' Questions

1. It seems now that everywhere Jesus goes, trouble arises and arguments break out. Is Jesus causing trouble? **See Luke 12:51-53.** What does Scripture have to say about the world's reaction to the Son of God? **Read John 1:11-12; Acts 4:25b-26; 1 Corinthians 2:14.**

2. Does Christ's message still cause division and uproar today? _____ If so, why? **Read 1 John 3:13; John 15:18-19; Matthew 10:16-22 and Ephesians 6:12.**

3. Once again the religious authorities were not able to apprehend Jesus because His _____ had not yet _____. **John 7:30; 8:20**

⁴⁸ "None of us religious authorities or Pharisees are believin' Him, are we? That ought to tell ya somethin'." (Hmmh!)

⁴⁹ They went on spoutin', "That mob of pilgrims, who don't know the Law, are accursed."

⁵⁰ Then ol' Nicodemus spoke up. (He was the one who had come to Jesus at night to have a talk. He liked Jesus.)

⁵¹ Nicodemus said, "Hold on fellas, our law don't allow us to condemn a man until it first hears from him and knows firsthand what he's up to."

⁵² Not takin' kindly to Nicodemus' words of caution, those that were already against Jesus sneered, "Well, what have we got here, another Galilean? Nothin' good ever comes from Galilee. Search the Scriptures for yourself, you'll see."

⁵³ Then everybody cleared the streets and went on home.

Thinkin' Questions

1. What are the religious leaders using as their excuse to oppose Jesus and His followers in **verse 49**? **Look in the Old Testament --Deuteronomy 27:26.**

2. What is the reaction of those against Jesus to Nicodemus' voice of reason? Look at **verse 52**.

3. Looks like the religious leaders are picking out only the Scriptures that support their own thinking. They must have missed **Isaiah 9:1-2**; also quoted in **Matthew 4:12-16**. Is this inappropriate way of approaching Scripture still practiced today?

4. What is Jesus' relationship to the Law? **Read Matthew 5:17-20; Luke 24:44; Romans 8:1-4; Romans 10:3-4 and Galatians 3:11-13 & 21-29.**

Chapter Eight

Ropin' the Truth

¹ Then Jesus headed off to the Mount of Olives. Seems that partic'lar place was one of His favorite spots to spend some time prayin'.

²· Early the next mornin' Jesus rode back to the Temple and all the folks were makin' their way to Him. He just sat right down and started teachin' again.

³ Weren't long 'til those scribes and Pharisees showed up again. This time they was draggin' along a woman they said to have caught in adultery and they throwed her down right in front of Jesus while He was teachin' the people.

⁴·⁵ They announced to Jesus, "Teacher, we done caught this woman with a man that ain't her husband. Now, abidin' by the Law, Moses said we are to stone such a woman. What do You got to say about that?"

⁶ Jesus knew they were testin' Him, trying to trip Him up so they could accuse Him of goin' against the Law. Jesus looked at the men and the woman without sayin' a word. Then He stooped down and started writin' in the dirt with His finger.

⁷·⁸ While He was a-writin', they kept on pushin' Him to give an answer. Jesus raised up then and spoke, "*Okay, any of you fellas that has never broken the Law in any fashion, you throw the first stone.*" He stooped down and started writin' some more stuff in the dirt.

⁹ I reckon their jaws dropped and they done saw what it was Jesus was a-writin' in the dirt. Startin' with the oldest, one-by-one they high-tailed it out of there until ever' last one of 'em was gone. It was just Jesus and the woman remainin' there.

¹⁰·¹¹ Then Jesus stood on up and asked her, "*Where are they? Is there anyone condemnin' you now?*" She answered, "No one, Lord." And Jesus told her straight, "*Neither do I condemn you ma'am. Go now, and don't be sinnin' from here on out.*"

Thinkin' Question

1. Jesus explained His relationship to the Law in **Matthew 5:17-20;** our relationship to the Law in **Matthew 5:27-30.** He reveals the greatest commandments of the Law in **Matthew 22:35-40**. Use the following page if needed to describe how Jesus demonstrates grace (**John 1:16-17**) in the above story without disregarding the Law. **Consider James 2:8-13.**

_____

_____

_____

_____

_____

_____

_____

_____

_____

_____

_____

_____

_____

Chapter 8   Just Thinkin

The 8th Chapter of John reminds us of an old west lynch mob. The chapter opens with some Pharisees planning to stone to death a woman caught in the act of adultery. It closes with Pharisees picking up rocks to stone Jesus. Truly there is a great contrast between the woman caught in adultery and Jesus. But both were subjected to the self-righteous judgment of the Pharisees. Rather than permitting the woman to be stoned, Jesus saw it as an opportunity to forgive her and a time for those who were accusing her to see their own sins and their own need for forgiveness (verse 7). Sin in God's eyes is a serious matter, but in His love He chooses to offer forgiveness; we have but to repent and receive it. Jesus didn't give in to the lynch mob but rather said to the woman: *"Where are they? Is there anyone condemnin' you now?"* She answered, "No one, Lord." And Jesus told her straight, *"Neither do I condemn you ma'am. Go now and don't be sinnin' from here on out."* John 8:10-11

¹² With that, Jesus just turned and began speakin' again to the crowd who was still there waitin' around for more teachin'. *"I am the Light of the World."* He said. *"Any of the fellas and gals who follow after Me won't ever walk in darkness, 'cause they will have the light of life."*

¹³ Now there was some more Pharisees hangin' around in the crowd still tryin' to cause trouble for Jesus wherever they could. I reckon they were plenty mad 'cause their little plot hadn't worked to trip Jesus up. One of them jumped up 'n snarled, *"You can't testify about Your own self and expect us to believe it!"*

¹⁴ Jesus spoke right up to the man, *"I know where y'all are goin' with this, but you don't know as much as ya think you do. Ya see, it's 'cause I know where I come from and where I'm goin' that I can testify about Myself and it is true. But y'all don't know where I come from and ya don't know where I'm goin' neither.*

Thinkin' Questions:

1. What does the term, *"Light of the world"* mean to you? **Read Luke 2:25-32; John 1:4-9; John 3:19-21; John 9:4-5 and John 12:35-36.**

2. What are some spiritual blessings that come with the light of Christ? **Look up the following Scriptures: John 12:44-46; Acts 26:16-18; 2 Corinthians 4:6; 1 Peter 2:9-10; 1 John 1:5-7; Ephesians 6:12-13 and Colossians 1:9-14.**

3. What does it mean for a person to *"walk in darkness"*? **See 1 John 2:9-11.**

4. **Isaiah 59:10** paints a dark picture. Do you recognize any similarities in our world today?_____ What does the darkness have for those who walk there? See the lists on the following page. **Look at Isaiah 5:20; also Isaiah 60:1.** What hope is there?

5. **In verse 14,** Jesus once again points out the blindness of the Pharisees. Why do you think this group of religious "experts" didn't recognize the Son of God? **See Matthew 23:23-28.**

Study the following characteristics with and without the "the Light of the world".

In the Light of Christ	In Spiritual Darkness or Night

- Experience presence of God in life
- Indwelling of the Holy Spirit
- Deliverance from spiritual darkness
- Work of God can be done thru us
- Understanding spiritual things
- Disables the power of satan
- Forgiveness and removal of guilt
- Sanctification (made holy) thru faith
- Knowledge of God's glory
- Fruit of the Spirit development
- Priesthood of the believer
- Freedom from fear
- Mercy received and given
- Fellowship with the other believers
- Cleansing from sin
- Love for others
- Ability to put on the armor of God
- Communion with God thru prayer
- Knowledge of God's will
- Guidance for a God-pleasing life
- Peace
- Joy in the Lord
- Contentment in all circumstances
- Power to overcome temptation
- Freedom from the law of sin & death
- Abundant Grace for living on earth
- Eternal Life with God
	- Absence of God in our lives
	- Work of God not done thru us
	- Lost/Deceived
	- Vulnerable to sin and death
	- Innocent are killed
	- Destructive actions seem normal
	- Unrighteousness
	- Stumbling in search of happiness
	- Denial of God
	- Power-seeking Oppression of the weak
	- Denial of truth
	- Resentment/Bitterness
	- Struggle with our own:
	   ○ Guilt
	   ○ Lies
	   ○ Injustice
	   ○ Dishonesty
	   ○ Mischief
	   ○ Deceitful schemes
	   ○ Violence
	   ○ Evil thoughts
	   ○ Compulsion for evil acts
	   ○ Unrest and lack of peace
	   ○ Dark Depression
	   ○ Growing discontent
	   ○ Severe Frustration
	   ○ Hate

References: John 9:4-5; Isaiah 5:20; Isaiah 59:1-15; Luke 22:53; John 1:4-9; John 3:19-21; John 12:35-36; John 12:46; 1 John 2:7-11; 1 Peter 2:9-10; Ephesians 5:8-14; Ephesians 6:12-13; Colossians 1:9-14; Psalms 27:1; Psalm 36:9; Acts 26:18; 2 Corinthians 4:6

There are other scriptures. Benefits of walking in the Light are endless. Write a few from your personal experience. _____

_____

_____

¹⁵ *Y'all judge by what you see thru your own natural eyes; I judge no one.*

¹⁶ *But on the other hand, if I did judge, My judgment is square; for I don't judge just for Myself, but My Father who sent Me, He is in on it, too.*

¹⁷ *For sure, your law reads that when two men give an account of somethin', then it is reckoned to be the truth.*

¹⁸ *So I'm tellin' y'all that I and My Father are both testifyin' about Me. That means it's plumb true accordin' to the Law."*

¹⁹ *With gritted teeth they said to Jesus, "So where is Your Father?" Jesus said, "Well, now that's where y'all just don't get it. Since you don't know Me, then you don't know My Father either. If you knew Me, then well, I reckon you would know Him, too."*

²⁰ By now Jesus was in the treasury of the Temple. There was plenty of deputies around, but just like before nobody nabbed Him 'cause His time for that had not come yet.

~——————~

Thinkin' Questions

1. Back in **John 8:13** the Pharisees accused Jesus of lying. They used a law stating that true testimony must be backed up by two witnesses. In **verse 18** what grounds does Jesus give for declaring His own testimony to be true according to law.

2. What hinders the Pharisees from knowing who Jesus is and believing in Him? **Read verse 19 above. Refer also to John 6:44-45.**

3. Describe the principle in **verse 19** that sets Christianity apart from all other religions? **See also Philippians 3:8-10 and I John 5:20.**

[21] Then He told them again, *"I'm gonna ride out and y'all are gonna be lookin' for Me. But you'll die in your sin, 'cause where I'm goin', you can't come."*

[22] So the Jews started speculatin' amongst themselves, "Y'all don't think He's gonna kill Himself, do you, since He's a-sayin' 'Where I am goin', y'all can't come?'"

[23] Jesus was tellin' 'em, *"Ya see, y'all are from here below; I come from above. Y'all are of this world; I am not from here!*

[24] *And since y'all are from this world, you sure will die in your sins unless you believe that I am the One sent to take away your sin."*

[25] So they were sayin' to Him, "Just who in the world are you then?" Jesus said to them, *"That's what I've been a-tryin' to tell you fellas from the start, haven't ya heard anything?"*

~~~

Thinkin' Questions

1. The Bible teaches that Jesus was born in Bethlehem of Judea. What was meant by Jesus' statement that He is from above and we are from below? **Read John 1:1-5; John 6:38; John 8:42; John 16:27-28; John 8:58; also Matthew 22:42-46 and Colossians 1:15-17.**

2. In **verses 21 & 24** Jesus states that ALL who don't believe and follow Him will die in their sins. Why can't a person turn from sin on their own and be a good person without believing in Jesus? **Look at the following Scriptures: Romans 3:10-23; Ephesians 2:8-9; Isaiah 64:6 and Proverbs 14:12.**

²⁶ *"I've got plenty I could say to y'all about the way things are around here, but He who sent Me has rightly planned out the words He wants Me to speak. I only say the words that I hear from Him; those are the words I'm speakin' to the world."*

²⁷ They still didn't get that Jesus was talkin' to 'em about His relation to God the Father.

²⁸ So Jesus told them this, *"When y'all lift up the Son of Man, then you will know that I am He, that is, the One you've been waitin' for. I don't do things on My own account. I just do what My Father has taught Me. Ya see, He's My Trail Boss.*

²⁹ *And He's right here with Me. He didn't send Me off to be here by My lonesome. So ya see, everything I do is accordin' to His likin'."*

³⁰ Now as Jesus was a-speakin' these things, a whole bunch of the folks around came to believe in Him. Yes-sir-ee, they did.

Thinkin' Questions

1. **In verses 26-29,** Jesus reminds us again that He speaks and acts not on His own initiative, but according to the will of the Father. **Read also John 5:30 and John 14:10.** Do we have the same opportunity Jesus had on earth to speak and act on the words and teachings of the Father? How is that? **Read John 8:47; John 14:26; John 16:13; Matthew 10:19-20; Acts 4:31; Acts 13:2-3; Romans 8:14-16 and 1 Corinthians 2:12-13.**

2. Jesus made it clear in **verse 29** that He is not alone. How about us? Look at **John 14:16-18 and Matthew 28:19-20.** Do you experience the presence of your *"Trail Boss"* with you at all times? In what ways?

3. What is the good news **in verse 30**?

31-32 And Jesus was a-tellin' the Jews who done believed in Him, *"If y'all will hang your hats in My word, then y'all are surely true wranglers in My outfit. And there's one thang for sure; with Me you rightly will know the truth, and the truth will set you free."*

33 Now them Pharisees were mighty confounded and they said to Jesus, "Well now, we ain't never been a slave to nobody, so how is it we will be set free?"

34 Jesus spoke up then and said, *"Y'all hear Me now, I'm shootin' straight with ya. Any of y'all who has ever sinned is a slave to his sins.*

35 *Ya see, a slave can't live in the house forever, 'cause it is not his house. But a son, well he can stay there as long as he wants.*

36 *So ya see, if the Son sets you free, well I reckon, you are sure 'nough free.*

37 *I know that y'all come from Abraham, still ya want to slaughter Me 'cause My word does not add up to what y'all want to believe.*

Thinkin' Questions

1. According to **verses 31-32** above, how does knowing Christ set us free? **Read Romans 7:6; Romans 5:1-2; Romans 8:1-2; Galatians 5:1,13-14 & 18; 2 Corinthians 3:17 and 1 Peter 2:13-17.**

2. How are we to live the Christian life in the freedom that Christ gives us? **Check out Romans 6:14-19 and 1 Peter 2:13-17.**

3. While living out our freedom in Christ, what responsibilities are reflected in the following verses? --**1 Corinthians 8:7-13 and 1 Corinthians 10:23-31; also Galatians 5:16-24.**

4. Under the new covenant, who are the *"children of Abraham"*? **Read Galatians 3:6-7, 21-29.**

[38] *I'm just tellin' y'all what I know 'cause I've seen all these things with My Father; but y'all do things that you heard from your own father. It's just not right."*

[39] *Well, that did it. "Abraham is our father!" they snarled. So then Jesus said to these fellas, "Okay then, if y'all come from Abraham, then do the things Abraham did.*

[40] *Y'all are lookin' to gun Me down, a Man who has done nothin' but tell y'all the truth from God Himself. Abraham would have no part of your schemes.*

[41] *You ornery ones are doin' the deeds of your father, alright." But now those fellas just kept on insistin' they was legitimate sayin', "God is our Father".*

[42] *But Jesus told 'em again straight, "If y'all were God's children for real, then you would be rightly fond of Me, 'cause I would be your kin. Ya see I came forth straight from God the Father. I didn't just decide to do this all by Myself. He sent Me here.*

[43] *Don't y'all understand My words? Can y'all not hear what I'm tellin' ya?*

[44-45] *Here's how it is: Everyone of y'all that's so against Me has the devil for his father. Y'all run to do the biddin' of your old pappy who's been a murderer from the very start. He doesn't stand anywhere near the truth 'cause there is no truth in him. Nothin' but lies come out of his mouth on account of that is what he is. He is a dirty rotten liar, the Father of Lies. That's why y'all don't like it when I tell you the rightful truth.*

[46-47] *Which one of y'all can find Me guilty of even one sin? Then why don't you believe My true words? Any fella or gal who belongs to God hears the words of God. Y'all don't hear His words because you are not His."*

Thinkin' Questions

1. What big lie did Satan use in the Garden of Eden to cause Eve to be tempted? **Read Genesis 3:1-5.**

2. Does the evil one still use the same lie today? What are some examples? **Examine 2 Corinthians 11:3-6 & 12-15 and 2 Thessalonians 2:9-12.**

3. Is there "absolute truth"? _____ **See John 17:19; John 18:37 and Romans 1:18.** Why is knowing and believing the truth important? **Read Matthew 24:4-5 & 24; also 2 Timothy 2:15 and 2 Timothy 4:2-4.**

⁴⁸ Well, those Pharisees were about to turn plumb wrong-side-out. They bowed up at Jesus again and said, "Ain't we correct in sayin' that You are a Samaritan and You have a devil?"

⁴⁹ Jesus looked at them square in the eyes and said, *"Let Me set the record straight here for all you folks. I don't have a demon. I honor My Father, but y'all dishonor Me.*

⁵⁰ *I do not look for glory for Myself. But there is One who gets the glory and He will judge.*

⁵¹ *This is the straight truth; every fella or gal that lives by My words will never die."*

⁵² Then those Jews who was opposin' blurted out, "Now we're dead level sure You're demon possessed. Ol' father Abraham's dead, the prophets all died; and You're a-sayin' if anybody keeps Your word, they're gonna live forever?"

⁵³ "Surely" they mocked, "You're not claimin' to be better than Abraham and the prophets, are You? Just who in blazes are You makin' Yourself out to be?"

⁵⁴ Jesus spoke up, *"If I give glory to Myself, that is nothin'. My Father, He gives Me glory; the One y'all are claimin' is your very own God.*

⁵⁵ *The honest truth is y'all don't even know Him. But I know Him; and if I was to agree with you and say that I didn't, well, that would make Me a liar just like you. But I'm tellin' ya I do know Him and I live by His Word.*

⁵⁶ *Don't you know that Abraham was mighty proud to see I was comin'. He saw Me alright and kicked up his heels with pure delight."*

⁵⁷ Well their jaws dropped with that one, and with a smirk they said, "You ain't even fifty yet, and You're braggin' that You've seen Abraham?"

⁵⁸ Then Jesus just told 'em plain out, *"Here's the real truth of the matter: I was and still am before Abraham was."*

⁵⁹ That done it! The scoundrels grabbed some rocks to throw at His head, but before they could get it done, Jesus had walked right out of the temple. Weren't the time for none of that just yet.

Thinkin' Question

1. According to Scripture, the Jews are God's chosen people. Does this guarantee them a home in heaven? _____ Why or why not?

2. What is Jesus saying to the Jewish religious leaders in **verses 47 & 55? Read Romans 3:9, 21-23 and Romans 10:11-13.** Write your thoughts on the following page…

Chapter Nine

A Blind Man Sees

¹ Now Jesus was ridin' the trail with His pardners when He saw a fella that had been blind his whole life. Jesus stopped and got down off His horse.

² His pardners were hankerin' to know so they asked Him, "How come he's like this? Did he sin or was it his ma and pa's sin that caused him to be born that way?"

³ Jesus told 'em, *"It weren't neither this man nor his folks that sinned; but it happened so that the works of God could be showed up in him.*

⁴ *We have to do the work of Him that sent Me while the sun is still a-shinin'; 'cause when night sets in, no one can work.*

⁵ *As long as I am in the world, I am the Light of the world."*

⁶ After He said that, He spat on the ground and rolled up a piece of mud made from His spit, and daubed the mud on the blind fella's eyes.

⁷ And then He told the man, *"Now, go over yonder to that Siloam pond."* So he went off and washed and when he came back he could see.

⁸ Well, there was a whole herd o' folks who had been seein' this man blind and beggin' his whole life; some of his own neighbors came along. "Ain't this the one we've known to be a blind beggar? Look at him now!" they said.

⁹ Some of them folks was sayin', "Nah, this can't be him, must be he just looks somethin' like him. Still some of 'em was insistin' it was him. The man just kept on tellin' 'em, "Hey, it's me! I'm the one!"

Thinkin' Questions

1. It was believed in Jesus' day that physical ailments were the direct result of someone's sin. It must have been an eye opener for His pardners to hear otherwise in **verse 3**. What does it mean that this man's blindness had a higher purpose? How does this translate to other serious illness and handicaps?

2. Jesus' compassion could not allow this man to remain blind when the Light of the world was passing by. Why do you think Jesus chose to heal him in the way that He did, with the mud and the washing?

3. Explain what **verse 4** means to you. Is the sun still shining today? **Read 2 Corinthians 4:3-6; Ephesians 5:8-14 and 1 John 1:5-7.**

Notes

¹⁰ So they started askin' him, "So how is it you can see now? What happened to ya?"

¹¹ He told 'em, "That Feller named Jesus made some mud and plastered it on my eyes. He told me, 'Go to Siloam 'n wash' so that's what I did, and now I can see."

¹² Then they asked him, "Okay, so where's He now?" He answered them, "Well now I don't rightly know."

¹³ So they wrangled him over to show him to the Pharisees --this man who used to be blind.

¹⁴ It just so happened it was the Sabbath Day when Jesus made the daub of mud and opened the blind man's eyes. Here we go again.

¹⁵ Same as the others, the Pharisees started in askin' the man how he got his sight. He told them just how it happened, "He put mud on my eyes; I washed and now I see."

¹⁶ "Ohho," some of the Pharisees were saying, "This Healer can't be from God 'cause He don't keep the Sabbath." But others were askin', "So how's it possible if He's a sinner that He can perform such miracles?" And so there resulted another ruckus amongst 'em.

¹⁷ So they asked the blind man again, "What do ya know about this Dude, seein' as how He caused you to see and all?" And he told 'em "Why, He's a prophet, that's what. There ain't no doubt about it!"

Chapter 9 Just Thinkin

A lone cowboy traveling through unknown territory never looked directly into his campfire because his eyesight would be obscured to identify the source of any strange sounds in the night. In the 9th chapter of John we read about a man whose eyesight had been obscured from birth. All his life he lived in a dark world but that changed when Jesus healed him. However, it was more than physical sight the man received, he also gained spiritual sight. That is seen in four progressive steps when the man was answering the Pharisees questions about how and by Whom he was healed. First he said "that Feller named Jesus" healed me (verse 11). Later he called Jesus a "prophet" (verse 17). After some more interrogation by the Pharisees the man stated his belief that Jesus was "from God" (verse 33). And then in a conversation with Jesus the formerly blind man takes a final step of belief when he openly declares Jesus as "Lord" (verses 35-38). It is a great miracle when physically blind eyes are opened. But perhaps the greater need is for those who are blind to the truths of God and His great love. They like this blind man need healing to receive spiritual sight into the glorious salvation of the Lord our God. *There's one thing I do know; I was blind but now I see.* John 9:25

Thinkin' Questions

1. Why do you think folks were questioning the man regarding *how* he was healed? Why did they take him to the Pharisees?

2. What did the Sabbath have to do with the healing of the blind man? How would the Pharisees use that against Jesus?

3. What's the difference in the way the healed man refers to Jesus in **vs 11** and **17**? Do you see a progression in the man's realization of who Jesus is? Explain.

¹⁸ Then those Pharisees questioned if he had been born blind at all, and didn't believe he was just now seein' for the first time. They sent for his folks.

¹⁹ When his ma and pa showed up, they asked 'em, "Is this here your son? Is this the one you say was born blind? How is it that he can see?"

²⁰⁻²¹ His pa and ma said, "We know by sure reckonin' this here is our boy and sure 'nough he was born blind; but how he is able to see now, we ain't got no idea; we are dumfounded. Why don't y'all ask him since he's a grown man and speaks for hisself."

²² Truth is this fella's folks were plumb scared of the Jews; they knew if anybody fessed up that Jesus was the Christ, they'd be booted right out of the church.

²³ On account of they was afraid, they just put it out there on their son 'cause He was already sayin' it for hisself.

²⁴ Then they went and rounded up the man again for the second time and said to him, "Give glory to God; we figure this Man is a sinner who done healed you."

²⁵ He told 'em straight out, "I don't know if He is a sinner, but there's one thing I do know; I was blind but now I see, that's all."

²⁶ Now them Pharisees was leanin' on him alright. They put the questions to him again, "Just tell us what in blazes He did to ya. How did He open your eyes?"

²⁷ He said to em', "I done already told y'all that. Do ya want to hear it again? Maybe y'all are hankerin' to be His pardners, too, and have Him as your Trail Boss!"

²⁸ Well they about choked on that one. "You're His pardner, not us! We follow the teachings of Moses," they snarled.

Thinkin' Questions

1. The Pharisees are supposed to be the most religious people in the country, most dedicated and devoted Jews. Why are they so angry about this wonderful miracle that has taken place in this man's life?

2. Doesn't religion bring a person closer to God? Can it actually be a hindrance? How? **Read Matthew 23:1-28 and James 1:26-27.**

Notes

[29] "We for sure know that God talked to Moses; but this here Fella, we don't even know where He came from."

[30] The man who now had his sight said to them, "Ain't that somethin'? Y'all don't' have no notion where He comes from, and yet He done opened my eyes."

[31] He went on a-tellin' them a thing or two, "Okay, we know that God don't hear the prayers of sinners; but if a fella fears God and does His biddin', well now, He'll hear him.

[32-33] From the beginnin', it ain't never happened before that somebody opened the eyes of a person who was born blind. If this Man weren't from God, He couldn't do that or nothin' else."

[34] Now there had to be some folks around there laughin' their behinds off by this time. Them Pharisees were completely confounded and mad as hornets! They gritted their teeth and snarled at him, "You was born in sin all the way. You ain't never been any good and you're tryin' to teach us?" Then they gave him the boot right out of the ol' synagogue, yes-sir-ee!

[35] Jesus heard about all that took place, so He went a-lookin' for the man. When He found him, He asked him straight out, *"Do you believe in the Son of Man?"*

[36] And he said, "Tell me who He is, Lord, so that I can believe in Him."

[37] Jesus said, *"Mister, you've done already met Him; He is the One who is talkin' to ya right now."*

[38] The man said, "Whew, Lord, I believe!" And right then and there he worshiped Jesus.

[39] Jesus told him, *"I came into this world to set things right. Those who don't see will see, and those who ought to be seein' will sure 'nough be blind."*

[40] Some of them Pharisees what were hangin' 'round heard that and said to Him, "So we're not blind too, are we?"

[41] Jesus told 'em straight, *"If y'all knew how blind you are, ya wouldn't have any sin; but seein' as how y'all say that you see, well, your sin is still there."*

Thinkin' Questions

1. In **verses 31-34,** what has made the Pharisees so angry with the man healed?

2. As Jesus reveals Himself in **verse 37**, what now is the man's belief and what is his response to Jesus in **verse 38**?

3. Review again what Jesus says about the blindness of the Pharisees and others today. **Read Matthew 23:16-17 & 23-26; Luke 6:39-42; also 2 Corinthians 4:4.**

Chapter Ten

The Good Shepherd

¹⁻² Jesus spoke up, *"Y'all listen to the true things I'm tellin' ya. Ya see, if some cowpoke sneaks into the sheepfold without walkin' in through the gate; well, he is a thief and a scoundrel up to no good. Ya see, the shepherd of the sheep will come on in through the gate honest like.*

³ *It is to that fella that the gatekeeper will open the gate, and his sheep done recognize his voice and he knows every one of 'em by name and leads 'em out.*

⁴ *And when he's gathered up all his own sheep, he walks ahead of them and they follow him 'cause they know his voice.*

⁵ *The sheep won't follow a stranger. No-sir-ee, they will all run off from him 'cause they don't know his voice."*

⁶ Those who were there just didn't understand what Jesus was saying to 'em, ya know. They didn't get it.

⁷ So Jesus told 'em straight out, *"C'mon, y'all listen up; I'm shootin' straight with ya. I am the Gate to the sheep.*

⁸ *All the others who have come along makin' claims to be Messiah are thieves and robbers tryin' to lead y'all astray. But those who are Mine didn't listen to them. I am here now."*

⁹ Jesus went on a-tellin' 'em, *"I am the Gate; if any fellow or gal enters through Me, they will have life forever, and will be free to go in and out safe and cared for.*

> Chapter 10   **ॐ**   Just Thinkin
>
> One summer I hired on to work for a dairy farmer. He had 96 Holstein cows to be milked twice a day. He knew each by name. The first day he introduced me to each one. When time came for the evening milking he would simply call out to them and they would come up from the pasture. I tried the same thing; cupped my hands to my mouth and called out the same way he did. But none of them moved; none started toward the milk barn. They just stood and looked at me. They did not know me; they did not recognize my voice. I was a stranger and they would not follow me.

Thinkin' Questions

1. In **verses 1-9**, Jesus is attempting to help folks understand how one can gain access to the Kingdom of God. In this illustration, what is the only way to get in? How do we know the voice of the True Shepherd? **Read John 14:6; John 17:3; Romans 5:1-2; Ephesians 2:18-19; 1 John 5:20.**

2. Jesus uses many word pictures to communicate His unchanging message. How does *"entering through the Gate"* in **verse 9** compare with other illustrations such as *"being born again"* in **John 3:3** and *"eating the true bread"* in **John 6:51** and *"drinking living water"* in **John 4:10; John 7:37.** Do you get it?

¹⁰ *The thief comes for no other reason but to steal and kill and tear up; I came so My own people will have life, and will be able to live life in a way that is good; one that is filled up with blessin's.*

¹¹ *And get this: I am the Good Shepherd; Ya see, the good shepherd lays down His life for the sheep.*

¹²⁻¹³ *A hired man is not truly the shepherd. The sheep don't belong to him. So, when he sees a wolf a-comin', he runs away. Then the wolf can come in and tear the sheep to pieces. The hired hand high-tails it 'cause he's just there for the pay. He doesn't care nothin' about the sheep.*

¹⁴ *I am the Good Shepherd, and I know My own and they know Me.*

¹⁵ *It's the same way My Father knows Me and I know My Father and I will surely lay down My life for the sheep.*

¹⁶ *I've got other sheep besides these that are in this fold. I'll be bringin' them along too. They will hear My voice and all My sheep will be gathered into one flock with one Shepherd.*

¹⁷ *My Father loves Me 'cause I come willin' to lay down My life so that I can take it up again.*

¹⁸ *"No fella on earth has the right to take My life, but I'm obliged to give it freely. I have the right to offer up My life and I have the right to take it back again I reckon. My Father gave Me His solemn word on this."*

Thinkin' Questions

1. What does **verse 10** reveal about imposters who claim to have another way to God? **Read Matthew 24:4-5, 11, 23-24. Consider also 2 Corinthians 11:13-15.**

2. How is Jesus able to say He is both the Gate to the sheepfold **(back in verse 7)** and also the *Good Shepherd* who knows His own sheep **(verse 14)? Refer to John 14:6; Isaiah 40:11 and Isaiah 55:9.**

3. Who might Jesus be referring to in **verse 16? See Luke 9:49-50; John 17:20-23 and also John 20:29.**

4. As the Good Shepherd is willing to give His life for the sheep, what further sets Jesus apart as the Son of God in **verses 17 & 18?**

[19] Now a ruckus rose up amongst the Jews again because Jesus was a-sayin' them things.

[20] The ones in the posse started mouthin' off again sayin', "He's got a demon inside of Him and it's driving Him crazy. Don't listen to Him!"

[21] A bunch of others shouted, "He ain't talkin' like somebody who's got a demon. There ain't no way a demon can open the eyes of a man who was born blind."

[22-23] There was another time on a winter day when there was a Feast of Dedication a-goin' on; Jesus was walkin' on Solomon's porch at the temple in Jerusalem.

[24-25] Them religious rascals surrounded Him and started houndin' Him again, "So how long are Ya gonna keep us guessin'? If You're really the Christ, why don't You just up and tell us?" Jesus said, *"I've already told y'all everything ya need to know and ya don't believe Me. I've performed miracles in My Father's name. That oughta speak for itself and tell ya who I am.*

[26-28] *But y'all don't believe because you're not one of My own outfit. Those who belong to Me hear My voice, and I know 'em, and they come along with Me; and I give them life everlastin' so they will never die. And for sure, nobody's gonna take 'em from My hand, no-sir-ee!*

Chapter 10 Just Thinkin

Some things are always the same. They never change. They are always predictable. The North Star is an example. It never changes, never moves from its place in the night sky. It is so predictable that ancient mariners as well as drovers pushing cattle to market in the post Civil War days depended upon it. The last thing the cook did before turning in for the night was point the tongue of his chuckwagon toward the North Star to keep them on course. The keeping Power of God is another of those things that never changes. Once a person has put his trust in Jesus Christ as personal Savior he/she is grasped in the strong hand of God never to be dropped, forsaken, forgotten, abandoned or snatched away. We are secured forever in the keeping power of God's love.

[29] *See, My Father has done given 'em to Me. He's greater than all; nobody can snatch His own from His hand.*

Thinkin' Questions -- Write your answers on following page.

1. This is not the first time Jesus is accused of *"having a demon".* Where do these accusations come from? **Refer back to John 8:42-47.**

2. Have you met folks today who are resistant to becoming part of Jesus' outfit as in **verse 26**? _____. Are there those today who claim to be part of God's flock, yet do not recognize the voice of Jesus? Why this rejection of the Son of God? **Refer back to John 1:5 and John 3:19-21; Matthew 7:21-23 and Luke 6:46.**

3. What assurance do we have according to **verses 28 & 29** once we become part of God's kingdom? **Read also Romans 8:1 and Romans 8:35-39.**

Note Page

1. _____

_____

_____

_____

2. _____

_____

_____

_____

3. _____

_____

_____

_____

³⁰ *That bein' said, you understand that I and the Father are One and the same."*

³¹ That riled up those Jews again alright. They looked around and got their hands on the biggest rocks they could find.

³² Jesus spoke up to 'em, *"Okay fellas, I've done shown you a whole passel of good works from the Father. Tell Me, which ones do y'all want to kill Me for?"*

³³ Them Jews was crazy mad for sure. They snarled at Jesus, "We ain't about to stone You for any good work You done. We are gonna kill You for blasphemy for sure. You ain't nothin' but a man and You make Yourself out to be God."

³⁴ Jesus reminded them, *"Don't y'all recollect even the Psalm writer in Scripture (Psalm 82:6) called human judges gods? (--Note the little "g" therefore not referring to deity.)*

³⁵ *I reckon they were called gods 'cause God gave them His message and sent them to do His work. Scripture can't be wrong then, so watch what you're doin'.*

³⁶ *I reckon you insult Me by sayin' 'You are blaspheming' because I said 'I am the Son of God who the Father set apart and sent into the world'. It is y'all who blaspheme by accusin' Me.*

³⁷⁻³⁸ *If I am not doin' the work of My Father, then don't believe Me; But if I get the work done My Father sent Me to do, believe the works even if you're still a-doubtin' who I am. That way, you'll come to see the Father is in Me, and I am in the Father."*

³⁹ Now those folks who was against Jesus didn't take kindly to His words. Once again they tried to take Him, but He walked on out away from them 'cause it still weren't time for that.

⁴⁰ Jesus rode out, back on the other side of the Jordan river where ol' John had first started baptizin'. He made camp there for awhile.

⁴¹⁻⁴² Weren't long before His followers found Him and started comin' out to Him again. Folks were a-sayin', "John didn't perform no signs, but for sure, everything he said about this Man is the truth." And a passel more people believed in Jesus right there at His campsite.

Thinkin' Question

1. Declaring His deity to the Jewish religious leaders was certain to enrage them **(verses 30-33)**. Yet Jesus keeps trying to get through to them. How did Jesus use Scripture to reason with them and make them think in **verses 34-35**?

Chapter Eleven

Raisin' Up a Dead Man

¹ Now it happened that Jesus had a good buddy who lived not far from Jerusalem who fell sick. This fella's name was Lazarus. He resided in the little ol' town of Bethany with his two sisters, Mary and Martha. They were all real good friends of Jesus.

² Mary was the very one who poured perfume on Jesus' feet and wiped it off with her hair. She done realized for sure who Jesus was. It was her brother Lazarus who was sick.

³ So a cowboy came a-ridin' up fast where Jesus was workin' and teachin'. He brought a message from the two sisters of Lazarus. The message read, "Lord, our brother and Your dear friend has fallen ill."

⁴ Jesus read the message and said, *"This sickness won't end with death. Lazarus has fallen sick for the purpose of bringin' glory to God; and so the Son of God can be glorified by it too."*

⁵ Ya see, Jesus had a high regard for Lazarus. He loved his sisters, Mary and Martha, too. There was more going on here for all their sakes.

⁶⁻⁷ Seemed a little strange at the time, but after Jesus read the message that Lazarus was sick, He stayed where He was two more days . . . then said to His pardners, *"Let's saddle up and ride back to Judea where Lazarus' family is."*

⁸ His partners said, "Boss, the Jews are tearing up the ground tryin' to find You 'cause they want to string You up. Are You right sure You want to be goin' back there again?"

⁹ Jesus told 'em this: *"Aren't there twelve hours of daylight most days? If a fella or gal is a-walkin' in broad daylight, they won't stumble or trip 'cause they see by the light of this world.*

¹⁰ *But don't ya know that if anybody walks in the night he's gonna trip and fall 'cause the light's not in him."*

Thinkin' Questions

1. What does **verse 3** reveal about Mary & Martha's relationship to Jesus and about their faith in Him? What does the message not say?

2. Why do you suppose Jesus did not go to His friends right away, but waited two more days (**verse 6**)?

¹¹ Then Jesus just flat out told 'em, *"Our buddy Lazarus has fell asleep. I'm goin' in daylight and I'm goin' to wake him up."*

¹² Jesus' partners said, "Okay Boss, if he's just sleepin' then he'll wake up feelin' just fine, won't he? Ain't no need for us to go."

¹³ The truth is, Jesus was speakin' about his death, but his pardners thought he was talkin' 'bout just regular sleep.

¹⁴ So Jesus spelled it out, *"Lazarus is dead."*

¹⁵ *"And for your own sakes I'm glad I was not there 'cause I want y'all to believe. So saddle up… we're goin' to him now."*

¹⁶ Ol' Thomas, also known as the twin, spoke up and said, "Hey boys, let's ride with Him. If He dies we might as well die alongside Him."

¹⁷ When Jesus rode up, Lazarus was already dead and buried four days.

¹⁸ Y'all understand that Bethany weren't but 'bout' two miles from Jerusalem.

¹⁹ And a bunch of the Jews had come on out there to comfort Martha and Mary seein' as how their brother had passed.

Thinkin' Questions

1. Though Jesus and His disciples had apparently received no updates on His friend Lazarus, Jesus was fully aware that he had died. What does that say to us regarding Jesus awareness of us and whatever circumstances we are in?

2. As believers Jesus calls us His friends. What kind of friend is He? **Read John 15:13-15 and Luke 12:4-7.**

3. The disciples had reminded Jesus in **verse 8** that He is risking His life by going to Bethany so close to Jerusalem. What kind of friend does Thomas prove to be in **verse 16**?

²⁰ When Martha got word that Jesus was comin' she lit out to meet Him, leavin' Mary in the house.

²¹⁻²² Martha plainly told Jesus, "Lord, if You'd been here sooner my brother wouldn't have died. But now You're here. I reckon that whatever You ask, God will give You."

²³ Jesus told Martha, *"Your brother's gonna rise again."*

²⁴ And Martha answered Him, "I plumb believe that he's gonna rise again on that last day like You told us."

²⁵⁻²⁶ Then Jesus did sure 'nough proclaim to Miss Martha. He said to her, *"I am the resurrection and the life; anyone who believes in Me will live even when he dies. And don't ya know that everyone who lives and believes in Me will never die. Do you believe this, Martha?"*

²⁷ She answered Jesus, "Yep Lord, I reckon I believe by faith that You are the Christ, the Son of God, the very One who comes into this world."

Thinkin' Questions

1. Putting yourself in Martha's sandals, what do you think she was conveying in her initial words to Jesus in **verse 21**?

2. In the conversation between Jesus and Martha in **verses 22-27**, what do you think Jesus is trying to do for Martha?

3. Martha may have thought Jesus was too late to heal her brother, but what beliefs does she profess with certainty?

4. Write down your own firm beliefs regarding Jesus Christ. Also write down the things you struggle with and make them a matter of prayer.

<u>Assurances in faith</u> | <u>Struggles & Doubts</u>

²⁸ Then Martha made her way back to the house to get her sister, Mary. She whispered to her real quiet like, "The Teacher is here and He's askin' about ya."

²⁹ As soon as Mary heard it, she was up and a-runnin' to Jesus, yes-sir-ee!

³⁰ Jesus hadn't come on into town yet. He was still a-waitin' in the very place where Martha had met up with Him.

³¹ Now, all of the neighbors and friends were in the house with Mary tryin' to comfort her. When they saw her get up and run off, they followed her 'cause they thought she was goin' to weep at Lazarus' grave.

³² But Mary was lookin' for Jesus where Martha had told her. When she saw Him, she fell at His feet all upset and cryin', "Lord, if You had only come sooner my brother wouldn't have died. You could've healed him!"

³³ When Jesus saw Mary cryin' with her heart so torn up; and seein' her friends and family with her sorrowin' so, He was deeply moved! He was troubled awful in His spirit to see 'em like that, and Mary so torn up."

Chapter 11 Just Thinkin

The shortest verse in the Bible! But it paints a huge emotional picture: *"Jesus wept."* How strange that we have fostered the idea that strong men don't cry. My grandfather was a strong man, a cowboy's cowboy. As a young man he worked as a drover helping to push cattle on some of the great trail drives to railheads in the north. If ever there was a man you could call strong, it was my grand-daddy and yet he was tender with a soft heart and strong emotion. Jesus too was strong, a man's man and yet we see Him weeping at the graveside of His dear friend, Lazarus. In *The Living Insights Study Bible* p. 1132, Charles Swindoll writes "Tears have a language all their own, a tongue that needs no interpreter."

³⁴ Jesus asked 'em, "Where is he? Where did you lay him to rest?" And they said to Him, "Lord, just follow us over yonder and we'll show Ya."

³⁵ Then Jesus wept too.

³⁶ So this crowd of Jews were a-sayin', "Look, He really loved His friend!"

Thinkin' Questions

1. What can we learn from Jesus' encounter with Martha and Mary regarding the Lord's responses to our own heartbreak and sorrow?

2. Jesus had known the moment Lazarus had died and where he had been buried. Why do you suppose He asked the question in **verse 34** and why does He allow Mary and the others to lead <u>Him</u> to the tomb?

[37] But some of 'em said, "Didn't He heal a blind man? Why in the world couldn't He have kept His good friend from dyin'?"

[38] Now Jesus came on up to the tomb a-feelin' mighty grieved for His buddy, Lazarus, and his family. The place where they had laid him was a cave and the opening was covered over with a large rock.

[39] Jesus said, *"Y'all take away the rock."* Martha was mortified, sayin' to Jesus, "Lord, he's been dead and buried for four days! There'll be an awful bad stench!"

[40] Jesus said to her, *"Martha, remember what I said to you back yonder, that if you believe, you will see the glory of God?"*

[41-42] So a bunch of men moved that rock out of the way of the entrance to the cave. Then Jesus lifted up His eyes to heaven and prayed right out loud, *"Father, I thank You right now that You have heard Me. I know You always hear Me; but its 'cause o' these people standin' around here that I'm a-sayin' it so they might believe that You sent Me."*

[43] After He had finished prayin', Jesus hollered out with a loud voice, *"Lazarus, come on outta there!"*

[44] And what do ya know! Lazarus, the fella who had died, came out of the grave still all tied up in them grave clothes so he could hardly move; even his face was bound up. Jesus said, *"Y'all, untie him and let him go."*

Thinkin' Questions

1. Do you sometimes question God's actions or seemingly lack of action like the folks in **verse 37**? _____ What is an appropriate way to do that as one of His own? Perhaps the answer is found in the Old Testament book of Job. **Read Job 21:4 & 22; Job 40:1-5 and finally Job's words in Job 19:25.**

2. How does Jesus respond to Martha when she worries in **verses 39-40**?

3. Prior to calling Lazarus forth from the grave Jesus publicly thanked God, the Father, in advance for what He was about to do? What does this say to us about faith expressed in our prayer life?

4. What kind of power is demonstrated in the raising of Lazarus? What assurance can we take away from this event?

[45] Now them Jewish folks who had come to pay their respects and comfort Mary and Martha saw what Jesus had done. A whole herd of 'em believed in Jesus that day, yes-sir-ee.

[46] Well, but don't ya know, some of them fellers skedaddled to the Pharisees and reported to 'em that Jesus had done raised a man from the dead.

[47] When they had heard all about it, the religious deputy fellas called together a committee. The chief religious honchos of them days was a-wringin' their hands sayin', "This Fella's been goin' around performin' a lot of signs and miracles. Now He's raisin' people from the dead! What in blazes are we gonna do?

[48] If we let Him carry on like this, everybody will believe in Him and our sweet deal with the Romans will go by the wayside."

[49] But then ol' Caiaphas spoke up. He was the high priest for that year. Caiaphas said, "Y'all don't know nothin' at all.

[50] And y'all don't reckon neither that it is more fittin' that one man should die rather than for the whole nation to be wiped out."

[51] Now here's the deal: Ol' Caiaphas didn't come out with that on his own. It was the Spirit's doin' on account of he was high priest that year. For that reason, it was prophesied out of his mouth that Jesus was gonna die for the nation.

[52] And not just for the Jews, but He would be roundin' up all God's children who were scattered all over the ranges of this world.

Thinkin' Questions

1. Seems in **verse 47** there was an official meeting held to devise a plan to thwart the message of Jesus Christ. List some ways this still goes on today.

2. We know that the high priest, Caiaphas, is not a believer. How is it that the Spirit of God used him in **verse 50** to prophesy such truth? **Read Romans 9:17-18; Numbers 22:21-23 & 28-31; Luke 19:39-40.**

3. Have you ever witnessed God using non-believers to accomplish His purposes? Write down that experience. Use the following page if needed.

Note Page

[53] From that day on, them religious Jews and their chiefs were a-plottin' to kill Jesus and waitin' for their chance.

[54] So Jesus didn't ride amongst the Jews out in public anymore. He made His way to the country out toward the wilderness. There was a town there called Ephraim. He stayed on there with His pardners for a spell.

[55] After awhile, it was gettin' close to the Passover again. A lot of folks was going up from the country to Jerusalem to get themselves pur-ee-fied for the holy week.

[56] Those religious scoundrels who were lookin' for Jesus, were a-talkin' about Him while they were in the temple, "Do ya think He's gonna show up at the Passover?"

[57] 'Wanted' posters were handed out by the chief priests and them high-and-mighty Pharisees. They was orderin' that if anyone knew the whereabouts of Jesus, he was to report it right away so they could nab Him.

Thinkin' Questions

1. At times in Scripture we see Jesus withdraw alone or with His disciples. What is the purpose of these retreats? **Read Mark 4:35-38; Mark 6:30-31; Luke 5:16; Matthew 14:13 & 23; Matthew 26:42-44.**

2. If we are attempting to serve Christ with our lives, how important is it that we spend time alone with Him to rest and pray and also in the fellowship of other believers for prayer and refreshing of our spirits?

3. If you are trying to live your life for God, and you are not carving out those times of retreat from the world, pray about that now and write down a prayer that you can refer back to over and again to make this a priority.

Chapter Twelve

Stayin' on the Trail

¹ Right near a week before the big Passover shindig, Jesus rode into Bethany. That was the town where Lazarus lived, the fella Jesus had raised up from the dead.

² They put on a big spread for Jesus. Miss Martha, she was dishin' out the grub. Lazarus was one of 'em who was eatin' there at the table with Jesus.

³ Then Miss Mary come up with somethin' like a pint jar of fine perfume and poured it out all over Jesus' feet. She began to wipe His feet with her hair. The whole house got filled up with the sweet smell of Mary's perfume.

⁴ But one of Jesus' pardners, ol' Judas Iscariot, who done already had a mind to backstab Jesus, he started in complainin'.

⁵ He grumbled sayin', "That stuff she's a-wastin' is worth a full years wranglin'! Why weren't it sold and the money give out to the poor?"

⁶ Now he weren't sayin' that 'cause he gave a hoot about the poor. Ol' Judas kept the money box, don't ya see, with all their money for expenses. He liked to skim some off for hisself when nobody was lookin'. He was a no good thief for sure.

⁷ Jesus said, *"Leave her alone now. It's right and proper for her to do this thing. She's been a-keepin' this for My burial.*

⁸ *You've always got the poor amongst ya, but y'all don't always have Me."*

Thinkin' Questions

1. Jesus knew His time on earth was growing short. He knew what lay ahead of Him in Jerusalem. He chose to spend this time with close friends who believed in Him. When we face challenges and grief in our Christian walk of faith and need spiritual support, who should we go to? Is it always family? **Read Acts 4:23-30; Acts 12:5-12; John 21:1-3; Mark 3:31-35.**

2. In the scene described above in **John 12:1-8**, Martha & Mary both express love for Jesus in different ways. In our relationship to Jesus, what are some ways we can express our love for Him? **Read Matthew 25:35-40 and Romans 12:9-13; also 1 John 5:3 and 1 Corinthians 13:4-7.**

[9] Before the week was out, a whole mob of folks found out Jesus was in town. They showed up too, and not just to see Jesus neither; but thinkin' they might get a good look at Lazarus, the one back from the dead.

[10] And the chief religious honchos who were after Jesus, well they was makin' plans to ambush Lazarus too!

[11] Because on account of Lazarus' a whole passel of them Jewish folk were believin' in Jesus and followin' after Him.

[12] The day came for Jesus to ride on into Jerusalem. The huge herd of folks who had come for the Passover got wind that Jesus was a-comin'.

[13] They all were pullin' branches off the palm trees and runnin' out on the road to meet Jesus. All along the trail they was a-wavin' them palm branches. They began shoutin', "Hosanna! Blessed is He who comes in the name of the Lord, the King of Israel!" (Psalms 118:22-27).

[14-15] Jesus done found a donkey's foal and got on it; 'cause ya see, it was written already in the Good Book, "Fear not Daughter of Zion. Behold your King is comin' seated on a donkey's colt" (Zechariah 9:9).

[16] Jesus' pardners didn't understand it all just then. But after Jesus was raised back up to His glory, they recollected them things what was written about Him. They reckoned they had done the very things to Him that was prophesied in the Scriptures.

Chapter 12 ❧❧ Just Thinkin

The opening of a rodeo is exciting and colorful. It is called The Grand Entry. Participants ride into the arena on horses, rodeo dignitaries are introduced, the slate of events is announced and the American flag is unfurled by a high-flying rider circling the arena. Fireworks may be exploded. It is an exuberant pageantry celebrating events that are about to happen. The Bible describes the day when Jesus rode into Jerusalem seated on a donkey's colt. Crowds gathered to shout "Hosanna!" and proclaim Him as King. Known as The Triumphal Entry it was a colorful and exciting display; a celebration praising Jesus! In reality it was a picture of another entry Jesus would most like to make into the lives of all who will receive Him by faith. What a cause for celebration it is when He is proclaimed forever as King and Lord in a willing and believing heart!

❧❧

---

[17] Now those folks who was with Jesus when He called Lazarus back from the dead were spreadin' the word 'bout Jesus for sure.

[18] Ya see, that's why all those big crowds of folks went out to see Jesus that day. They had done heard what He done.

Thinkin' Questions

1. How does the reason given in **verse 18** for Jesus' popularity in the scene above compare to His purpose for coming to walk amongst us?

2. Do people still seek Jesus for reasons that miss the purpose of His coming? _____ List a few.

¹⁹ Now them self righteous religious know-it-alls who was tryin' to get Jesus, they figured their schemes weren't workin'. "Look," they said, "Plumb near everybody's goin' out after Him."

²⁰ Now it so happened there was some Greek fellas amongst those who had come to worship at the feast of Passover.

²¹ These men cornered Philip, the pardner from Bethsaida of Galilee, and was a-sayin' to him, "Mister, we'd like to see Jesus."

²² Well ol 'Philip hightailed it to Andrew and told him what those Greek fellas was wantin'. The both of 'em was thinkin' they best let Jesus know. So they came and told Jesus about the Greeks who were askin' to see Him.

²³ This must have been some kind of personal signal for Jesus, 'cause right then He said, *"The hour has come for the Son of Man to be glorified.*

²⁴ *Listen up pardners! I'm tellin' ya straight. A seed grain of wheat has to fall to the earth and die so it can produce more wheat. If it's never planted, it'll always be just a single grain.*

²⁵ *Whoever loves his life will end up losing it for sure; but whoever is willin' to give up his life in this world, that cowboy or cowgirl will have life of the everlastin' kind.*

²⁶ *If anyone comes into My outfit, he will ride the trail with Me and wherever My trail goes, My drovers and wranglers will go too. If anyone does My biddin', well, My Father is gonna favor him for sure.*

²⁷ *Now I'm mighty troubled in My soul on account of what's comin'. Part of Me wants to say, 'Father, spare Me from the sufferin' that's about to come on Me.' But I reckon this is the very thing that I came for."*

Thinkin' Questions

1. The religious leaders realized that the events taking place were beyond their control. Who was in control?

2. The message from the Greeks in **verse 21** apparently gave Jesus full assurance that He had entered into the final phase of His mission. What is He trying to explain to His disciples in the illustration of the wheat in **verses 24 & 26**?

3. In spite of the grief already in His soul regarding what was ahead, Jesus continued on. What does this say to us in times of conflict and persecution when we know we are being obedient to God? **Read Romans 5:3-5; James 5:10-11; 2 Peter 1:5-8; 2 Corinthians 4:7-10; Romans 8:37-39 and 1 Peter 4:12-13.**

²⁸ *"Father, whatever it takes, give glory to Your name."* Then a voice rumbled out of heaven: **"I have glorified it and will glorify it again."**

²⁹ Now some of the folks standin' nearby said that it had thundered. But others said, "No, it were an angel what spoke to Him."

³⁰ Jesus told 'em, *"That voice that y'all heard wasn't on My account, but it was for your sakes.*

³¹ *Judgment is now on this world and the ruler of this world is gonna be knocked off his horse, yes-sir-ee, knocked right out of his saddle.*

³² *And when I am lifted up from the earth, then I will draw all folks to Myself; yes-sir-ee, each and every one."*

³³ Jesus was sayin' that, in particular, to let us know just how He was gonna die.

³⁴ Now talk was gettin' mighty serious and folks were puzzlin' over it. They said to Jesus, "Wait a minute! Our teachin' says when Messiah comes He's gonna stay forever; so how come You say the Son of Man has to be lifted up'? And just who in thunderation is this Son of Man?"

Chapter 12 Just Thinkin

My granddaddy told me many stories about his experiences as a drover on the old trail drives. He described how they dreaded the dark nights because in darkness the cattle were easily spooked. It didn't take much to spark a stampede. He told how on especially scary moonless nights they prayed for daylight. Jesus speaks of light, except He is not taking about light of day or light generated by the sun for He Himself is Light! Only Jesus can step into our life and give us peace instead of despair, hope instead of fear and life instead of death. He is the Light of the world.

³⁵ Jesus spoke up, *"For a spell longer y'all have the Light amongst ya. Walk while you have the Light so darkness won't overtake you here. The fella or gal who walks in darkness has no clue where he is headed.*

³⁶ *So long as y'all have the Light, believe in the Light so y'all can become the very offspring of the Light."* After Jesus had spoke these things He rode off by Hisself away from 'em.

Thinkin' Questions

1. Jesus said the *"voice"* heard in **verse 28** was not for Him, but for His followers. What do you think He meant by that? **Read Matthew 10:40. Then refer back to John 5:24 & 37.**

2. In response to the crowd, what is Jesus' concern expressed in **verses 35-36**? **Reference John 1:4; John 3:19-21 and John 8:12.**

[37] Now these folks had beheld Jesus doin' powerful miracles in front of their very own eyes, but a lot of 'em still wouldn't believe in Him.

[38] This happened so's to fulfill what the prophet Isaiah had wrote: "Lord, who has believed our message? And to whom has the strength of the Lord been revealed?" (Isaiah 53:1-3).

[39-40] Isaiah further said of them that wouldn't believe Jesus: "He has blinded their eyes and He made them even more stubborn in their heart, so they wouldn't see with their eyes and be perceivin' in their hearts, and get converted and be healed" (referring to Isaiah 6:10 paraphrased).

[41] Ol' Isaiah knew about Jesus and all His glory, yes-sir-ee. God done showed him and he told about it.

[42] But don't ya know, lots of the bosses up in the synagogue did happen to believe in Jesus, but they kept their mouth shut about it. They was a-feared them Pharisees would have 'em kicked out of the church.

[43] For ya see they was more worried about what men thought of 'em, rather than God.

Thinkin' Questions

1. In **verses 37-41** above, many of the folks who witnessed the miracles of Jesus and heard His preaching still did not believe in Him? Why do you think this was?

2. Many of the synagogue leaders who believed in Jesus kept it a secret. Persecution of Christians had already started. Is it still present in our world today? What about in our own country? Explain

3. Is it acceptable to have a secret faith in God? Does that work? **Read the following Scriptures and write what you think God is saying about this: Matthew 10:27-33; Luke 12:8-9; 2 Timothy 2:12; Matthew 6:6; also Matthew 6:17-18 and Luke 11:33.**

⁴⁴ So it was after bein' by Hisself awhile prayin' and ponderin' things, Jesus started preachin' again. He shouted out to all of 'em, *"Every one of ya who believes in Me is sure 'nough believin' in the One who sent Me.*

⁴⁵ *And if you're a-layin' eyes on Me, well you're lookin' at the One who done sent Me.*

⁴⁶ *I'm tryin' to tell y'all, I came as Light to this world so all y'all who will believe in Me won't have to walk in darkness any more.*

⁴⁷ *If any fella or gal hears what I'm sayin' and they can't swallow it, then it's not for Me to judge; I didn't come to judge the world. I came to save it.*

⁴⁸ *But y'all need to know that anybody who turns their back on Me with no regard for My words, for sure, will be judged. The very words I spoke to those folks will be what judges them in the last day.*

⁴⁹ *For ya see, the words I've been speakin' to y'all are not Mine. They are for sure God, the Father's very own words. He done sent Me for the purpose of speakin' His words so's y'all can understand. I been carryin' out My Father's mapped-out plan what to say and what to speak.*

⁵⁰ *And I know that if I carry through what My Father has done give Me to do, it will give everlastin' life to every one of ya who will take it to yourselves. So everything I say, I say it just like My Father told Me. That's the plain truth.*

Thinkin' Questions

1. One last time before the great crowds in Jerusalem, Jesus shouts out the message of who He is. In your own words what is the warning Jesus includes in the above passages?

2. Once again, what authority does Jesus give for His words in **verses 40-50**?

3. Put yourself in the crowd that day listening to Jesus appeal to the hearts and minds of those who can hear Him. **Write a simple prayer from your heart of belief and commitment to the Lord Jesus Christ.**

Chapter Thirteen

Devil in the Camp

¹ Jesus was ponderin' the fact that for sure His time was close. It was now the day before the big shindig, the Feast of the Passover. He would be departin' out of this world goin' to His Father real soon. He'd come to be mighty fond of all them folks who was His own. They had come to be like kin and mighty good friends in the world. It seemed like they were ready to follow Him to the very end. He loved 'em all, yes-sir-ee.

² At supper that night, the devil had done put the evil intent deep in the heart of ol' Judas Iscariot to betray Jesus. He was a-plottin' to put a knife right in Jesus' back, and Jesus was on to him for sure.

³ Jesus rightly knew that His own Pa, bein' God the Father, had done already given all and everything over to Him. He knew He had come from God sure 'nough and was goin' back home.

⁴⁻⁵ So Jesus got up from supper, took off His shirt, and girded up a towel 'round His britches. Right then, He filled Him up a washbowl and started in a-washin' His pardners feet and dryin' 'em off with the towel one by one.

⁶⁻⁹ But Peter said when his turn came, "Lord, why are You a-washin' my feet fer?" Jesus told him, *"You don't have the understandin' of it now, Peter, but hereafter you will understand it, don't ya see?"* But ol' Peter said, "Lord, it don't seem right. You ain't gonna wash my feet, never!" Jesus told him *"If I don't wash you, Peter, then you have no part with Me."* When Peter heard that, he plumb changed his tune, "Lord, in that case give not only my feet a good washin', but also my hands and my head!"

¹⁰ Jesus said, *"When a person has taken a bath, he is clean. He only needs to wash his feet after walkin' along the trail. You're clean, Peter, but not all of y'all are clean."*

¹¹ Ya see, Jesus knew which one of His pardners was goin' to turn Him over to them who was plottin' to kill Him. That there's why He said, *"Not all of y'all are clean."*

Thinkin' Questions

1. Jesus models for us an attitude of service and humility towards one another that He explains later, but there is a deeper lesson here, a foreshadowing of His work in our own lives. What do the following Scriptures say of washing and cleansing? **Read Isaiah 1:18; Psalm 51:1-2 & 7; 1 Corinthians 6:11; Titus 3:4-6.**

2. On the following page, list some ways Jesus still *"washes the feet"* of believers today? **Read 1 John 1:9; Ephesians 5:26-27; Psalm 103:1-5.**

Chapter Thirteen – Devil in the Camp

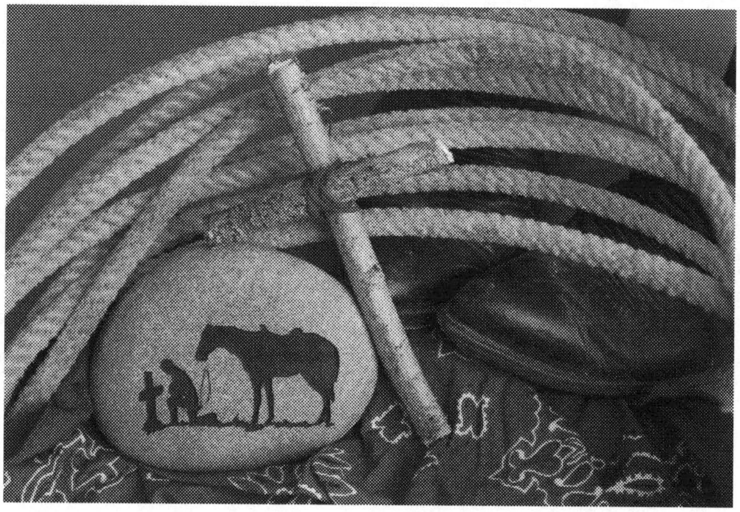

¹² After He was done washin' all their feet, He put His shirt back on and sat back at the table. Then He said to them, "Do y'all understand this thing I just did for you?

¹³ Y'all call Me Teacher and Lord and Boss, 'cause that's who I rightly am.

¹⁴ So if I, your Lord and Teacher and Boss done washed your feet, then for sure y'all ought to wash each other's feet.

¹⁵ Ya see, I done carried this out and showed ya so y'all can see how to be takin' care and havin' each other's back.

¹⁶ Its true, the cowboy in an outfit is not greater than the one in charge. And the one in charge is not greater than the one who put him in charge.

¹⁷ If y'all are understandin', then you'll be obliged to do like I've done showed ya.

¹⁸ But just now I'm not talkin' about every one of ya. I know My true pardners I've chose; but the Good Book has done prophesied, 'There's one who eats bread at My table who's gonna kick me in the teeth' (Psalm 41:9 paraphrase).

¹⁹ From here on out, I'm gonna be tellin' y'all things before they happen so that when somethin' comes along that stomps on your faith, you won't have any doubts about who I am.

²⁰ And another thing I want y'all to know is this: If I send somebody out in My name, the one who accepts him, also accepts Me. And when they accept Me, they'll get My Father who sent Me, right along with the deal, too."

Thinkin' Questions

1. In **verse 14**, Jesus makes a clear statement of how we as believers are to relate to one another. Foot washing was a customary expression of caring in those days; an humble act of love. How can we translate foot washing into today's lifestyle? List some ways we can demonstrate this attitude toward others today.

2. Jesus was grieved to say good-bye to His friends and to all who followed Him. In His final hours before His death He speaks important words to them to remember when things get tough. If you knew that God was going to take you home tomorrow, what important things would you say to those you care about? What would you say to them about your relationship with Jesus?

Notes

Chapter Thirteen – Devil in the Camp

²¹ Then Jesus pondered a bit and He was mighty troubled deep down. He spoke up from His heart and said, *"Believe Me when I tell ya! One of y'all is gonna' hand Me over."*

²² His pardners looked at each other dumfounded wonderin' which one of 'em it was He was talkin' about.

²³ They was all kicked back on the floor the way it was done in those days, and one of the younger fellas Jesus favored a bit was leanin' up against Him.

²⁴ So Peter motioned to this young cowboy and said, "Go ahead . . . ask Him who it is He's talkin' about."

²⁵ Sure 'nough, he leaned in closer to Jesus sayin', "Boss, won't Ya tell us who it is?"

²⁶ Jesus told him, *"I'm gonna' dip this piece of bread in the bowl here and the fella I give it to is the one."* So He took a piece of bread and dipped it and handed it to Judas Iscariot, the son of Simon.

²⁷ After Judas took the piece of bread, the old devil really got hold of him. Jesus looked him right in the eye and said, *"Do what you're gonna do, and do it quick."*

²⁸ The other pardners 'round the table had no idea why Jesus done said that to Judas.

²⁹ Some of 'em was thinkin' it was 'cause Judas was keepin' the money, and Jesus was sayin' to him, "Go and buy the stuff we're gonna need for the Passover"; or maybe that He wanted him to go give money to the poor.

³⁰ So after Judas had done taken the piece of bread Jesus gave him, he got up and left out. And now it was dark, real dark outside.

Chapter 13   Just Thinkin

Who has not felt the bitter sting of betrayal? If there was one thing a cowboy's life on the open range depended upon, it was the certainty that His friends on the trail were looking out for him. That cowboy riding by his side would have his back when a stampede erupted or a snake suddenly struck. Someone would be there if danger threatened from any direction. He was not alone. There were perils on the open range and no cowboy would leave another in harm's way. Yet that is exactly what happened to Jesus. One who had walked with Him for over three years, shared in His ministry, listened to His teaching, and had seen His miracles now will turn on Him as His enemies close in. The name of Judas Iscariot will always be associated with that of a traitor; the one who betrayed Jesus and handed Him over to His enemies for a handful of silver coins.

Thinkin' Questions

1. Evidently, the disciples did not have any clue that Judas was the traitor. What does the Bible have to say about imposters in our midst and how to deal with them? **Read Ezekiel 33:31; Isaiah 29:13; Matthew 7:15-16, 21-23 and Matthew 13:24-30, 37-41.**

2. Though some fake Christians will be revealed by their fruits, why is it not worthwhile for us to spend our time trying to wrangle out who is real and who is counterfeit? **Read 1 Samuel 16:7; Matthew 7:1-3; 2 Corinthians 10:12; also Ephesians 4:32. Write down your own understanding about this.**

[31-32] It was when Judas left, Jesus started sayin' some heavy stuff, *"Now the Son of Man is gonna be glorified. And God will receive glory through Him. For ya see, if God receives glory from the Son of Man, then He will also give glory to the Son from Himself. This is all about to start happenin' this very night.*

[33] *Hey listen kids, I'm not gonna be with y'all much longer. And y'all are gonna be lookin' for Me. But just like I told the Jews, I'm a-tellin' you now, 'Where I am goin' y'all can't come.'*

[34-35] *I'm givin' y'all a new command: I'm tellin' y'all to love each other. Just like I've loved you, y'all also love one another. Ya see, this is how folks are gonna know that y'all are My pardners if ya stick together and love and take care of each other."*

[36] Well 'ol Peter spoke up again like always and asked Him, "Lord, where are You headed off to?" Jesus told him, *"Where I'm goin', you can't go with Me just yet, but wait a spell and then you'll be able to come right along."*

[37] Peter argued, "But Boss, I don't see no reason why I can't ride along with You now. Everybody knows I would die 'fore I let anything happen to You."

[38] But Jesus answered him, *"Will you really die for Me? I tell you the truth, Pete, before the rooster crows you will say three times that you don't know Me at all."*

Comment: In some final words to His disciples, Jesus is trying to make them understand the most important thing is their love. This love is more than a strong emotion. Jesus is telling them straight out to put the other person first in His outfit even if it means sacrifice of one's own self. That is what love is, it is a choice, not a warm fuzzy feeling.

Thinkin' Questions

1. **Verses 31-32** indicate God will receive glory through what Jesus will do, and by glorifying His Father, Jesus will be glorified. How then do we, as God's children, glorify Him? How are we glorified? **Read 1 Chronicles 16:28-29; Psalm 50:23; Matthew 5:16; Luke 13:13; John 15:8; John 17:4; Psalm 8:4-5; 1 Peter 4:14.**

2. What does the Bible say about seeking our own glory? **Read Proverbs 25:27 and Matthew 6:2-4.**

3. Jesus' command to love goes above and beyond anything His pardners thought about before. In your own life, how does your love measure up to the love the Bible teaches us to have for one another? **Read John 15:11-17; 1 John 4:7-21.**

Chapter Fourteen

A New Trail Guide

[1]"I don't want y'all grievin' in your heart and hangin' your heads after I'm gone. Keep on believin' in God and believe in Me.

[2] There's plenty of room on My Father's spread; if it weren't so I would tell ya. I'm goin' there to get a place ready and fittin' for every single one of y'all.

[3] You can hang your hats on this; if I go to get a place ready for ya, I'll be a-ridin' on back My own self to fetch ya so where I am there y'all will be too.

[4] And y'all know the way to the place where I'm goin'."

[5] But Thomas said, "Boss, we don't know the trail You're a-takin' and no idea what direction You're headed; so how can we know the way?"

[6] Jesus said to him, "I am the way, the truth, and the life; there is only one trail to the Father and it's through Me."

Thinkin' Questions

1. Jesus is preparing His pardners for the severe test of their faith that is coming up the trail. He knows they will be confused and despaired after the cross. What assurance does He give them in **verses 2 & 3**?

Chapter 14 ❦ Just Thinkin

When I was eight it was my job to hold the gate open while my father and some other men unloaded cattle and pushed them into the corral. Sounds simple enough, just hold the gate. Well I was doing fine until a certain cow with a crooked horn began to eye me up as her target instead of the open gate. When she charged I left my post, the gate closed and the cattle scattered. Later my father asked me why I let the gate close? I told him that it was because "I got scared"! When Jesus told His disciples that He was the "way" to His Father, He was promising them and us that He would never let the gate to salvation close, no matter what. He Himself is the way and nothing will hinder anyone who desires to enter though Him into eternal life. In **Romans** the Apostle Paul talks about some great separators, then concludes that *"no created thing will be able to separate us from the love of God, which is in Christ Jesus our Lord."* Romans 8:39

1. According to **verse 6**, when we are lost and bewildered and don't know which way to go, Jesus is the _____.

1. When we are betrayed and confused and don't know what to believe, Jesus is the _____.

1. When we face fear and dread, depression and guilt, and need a reason to ride on, Jesus is the _____.

1. What does *"the way, the truth, and the life"* mean to you personally?

⁷ *"If y'all had truly known Me from the start, then you would have known My Father too. From here on out, y'all surely do know Him because you've seen Him."*

⁸ Philip said to Him, *"Lord, just show us the Father and that will plumb be all we need."*

⁹ Jesus told him, *"Philip, I've been with you for quite a spell now. How is it ya don't recognize Me? Anyone who has laid eyes on Me has for sure seen the Father; so how can ya say, 'show us the Father'?*

¹⁰ *Don't y'all get it that I am rightly in the Father, and the Father is in Me? All the words I've been sayin' to y'all and all the things I've been teachin'; none of that comes from Me. I don't come up with any of it on My own. The Father abidin' here in Me gives Me what to say and He carries out His work.*

¹¹ *Believe Me, y'all, when I say 'I am in the Father and He is in Me.' Or else believe Me because of the signs and the miracles.*

Chapter 14 ❧❧ Just Thinkin

Ever hear someone say, "That boy is the spitting image of his father?" That was certainly true of Jesus' relationship with His Father. And even more, Jesus, according to His own words was more than a spitting image; He and His Father were one and the same. So when anyone tells you that Jesus was merely a good man or a prophet or great teacher, then share with them what Jesus said to Philip in John 14:9.

❧❧❧

¹² *Trust Me when I tell ya that anybody who believes in Me will do the same works that I do. Fact is they'll do more works, on account I'm goin' to the Father.*

¹³ *And when you're a-prayin', whatever thing you ask in My Name I will do, so the Father can done be glorified through the Son.*

¹⁴ *Yes-sir-ee, y'all can ask Me anything in My name and I'll work it out.*

¹⁵ *That bein' said now, if ya love Me, you will keep My teachin'."*

～━━━～

Thinkin' Questions

1. According to **verse 9**, who does Jesus want us to recognize in Him?

2. According to **verse 10**, who is the origin of all Jesus' words and actions?

3. By assuring the disciples that He can answer their prayers leaves only one conclusion to be drawn by these Jewish men. Jesus is identifying Himself as _____.

16-17" I reckon to ask the Father, He'll send along to you another Trail Guide who will ride the trail with each one of you forever. I'm talkin' about the Spirit of Truth. The folks of this world won't let Him in, 'cause they can't see Him and don't know Him. But y'all know Him 'cause He'll be ridin' alongside you and will for sure be in you.

18 I'm not gonna leave you alone like orphaned doggie calves. I will come to ya.

19-20 Comin' up real soon, the folks of this world won't see Me no more. But you fellas and all them who know Me will see Me. And y'all will live because I live. Then you will know it for sure about Me bein' in My Father. And it will be the same, don't ya see, concernin' y'all and Me. Each one of ya will be in Me and I in you.

21 I know the ones who love Me and have My love in them. They hear My commands and do their best to live by 'em. Fellas and gals that love Me will have My Father's love in 'em. I will fill them up with God's love, and they'll know I am in their life."

22 So the other Judas (not Iscariot) asked Him, "Lord, what's takin' place that we will see You, but folks of the world won't?"

23 Jesus told him, "Just remember what I'm tellin' ya no matter what happens. If any fella or gal loves Me, they will keep My word; and My Father's love will be in them, and My Father and I will come and make Our homestead in each one.

24 By the same token, the ones who don't love Me won't even try to keep My words. The Father who sent Me is sayin' this."

Thinkin' Questions

1. Who does the Bible identify as the Spirit of Truth Jesus refers to in **verse 17**? **Look back and read John 7:37-39. Also read John 14:25-26; Acts 1:8 and 1 Corinthians 2:13-16.**

2. What characteristics and actions show up in our lives when we have a relationship with Jesus? --**Verses 21 & 23**

3. According to **verse 24** what is the evidence that a person does not know Christ? **Also read Galatians 5:16-17 & 19-21.**

4. Sin and falsehood may also exist behind an abundance of religion. Jesus can see right through piety and ritual. **Read Matthew 23:1-7,13-16, 23-28; Mark 12:38-40 and Luke 11:42-48 to see what Jesus says about that!**

[25] *"I have told y'all these things while ridin' the trail with you.*

[26] *Soon your new Trail Guide, the Holy Spirit, who the Father is gonna send along in My name; He will teach y'all all things and will bring to mind everything I have said to you.*

[27] *Peace is what I'm leavin' with y'all now. My own peace I'm givin' to each of ya; not the kind the world claims to sell. So don't fret none and don't be afraid.*

[28] *Y'all are troubled 'cause ya done heard Me say I was ridin' out without ya, and I will come back to ya later on. Ponder this: The way to show love for Me and put Me first is to be happy for Me 'cause I get to go home to My Father. He is greater than Me, don't ya see.*

[29] *Now fellas, I'm lettin' y'all in on this before it happens so's when it does take place you will believe.*

[30] *I won't be a-sayin' much more about this 'cause the devil is comin' to do his work. And he's got no part in Me;*

[31] *but so the folks of the world may know that I love the Father, I do everything right on, exactly as He tells Me. Get on up now, let's get goin'."*

Thinkin' Question

1. Jesus spoke of two kinds of "peace" in **verse 27**; His peace and the kind the world gives. What is the difference? **Helpful Scriptures include: Romans 5:2-5, 8-11; Romans 8:1-2, 5-6 & 28; also Philippians 4:6-7.**

Chapter Fifteen

Keep On Ridin'

¹⁻² As they were goin' along the trail, Jesus commenced teachin' again givin' His pardners somethin' more to ponder, *"Let Me put it to y'all this way: I am the True Vine and My Father is the Gardener. If there's a branch in Me that don't bear fruit; He culls it out and gets rid of it. And for the branches that are bearin', He prunes them back now and then so they will produce even more.*

³ *Y'all are in Me like a branch is in a vine 'cause you believe the words I spoke to ya.*

⁴ *Live in Me and I will live in you. Just like a branch can't bear fruit on its own, neither can y'all bear fruit unless you live in Me.*

⁵ *I am the Vine; y'all are the branches. The fellas and gals who live in Me and have Me livin' in them will bear wagonloads of fruit. But without Me, y'all can't do anything.*

⁶ *If a person chooses not to live in Me, just like a branch cut off from the vine, he or she will plumb wither and dry up. Dead branches aren't good for anything 'cept to be burned.*

⁷ *If you live in Me and My words are alive in ya, ask for anything that's fittin' and it will be done for ya.*

⁸ *Ya see, My Father is plumb honored when y'all are gettin' things done in My name, sure proof that y'all are My pardners.*

⁹ *I've loved y'all just like My Father done loved Me. It's mighty important that y'all keep ridin' in My love."*

———⟡———

Thinkin' Questions

Jesus is more concerned with *being* than *doing*. He doesn't only want us to serve Him, but to find our life in Him. Healthy fruit is a natural result of nourishment it receives from the vine. Take a few moments to ponder your own experience with Jesus.

1. What is the *"fruit"* that will continually grow in your life as a result of your relationship with Jesus Christ? **See Galatians 5:22-23.**

2. Take some time to examine your heart. Ask Jesus to be the source of who you are. Do you remember a time when the characteristics from **Galatians 5:22-23** were non-existent or not real for you? _____ Can you look back and realize the growth over time since you have been riding the trail with the Lord? _____ Write down some ways you have changed on a separate sheet of paper.

Notes

[10] "Y'all don't forget My commandments to ya, neither. That way, you can keep on ridin' and a-knowin' My love is in your hearts. Just like I kept My Father's commandments and did His work, ridin' all the time in His love.

[11] I keep sayin' these things to ya so y'all can know My blessin' deep down inside and be mighty pleased to overflowin'.

[12-14] If y'all haven't got this by now, let Me just tell ya again what I'm expectin' of ya. Here it is: The main thing is that y'all love one another just like I have loved you. There can't be no greater love than a fella givin' up his life for his friends. Y'all are My friends if ya love like that.

[15] I'm never gonna call y'all hired-hands 'cause a hired-hand has no idea what his trail boss is doin'. But I'm callin' ya friends 'cause I have told y'all everything that the Father done told Me to say since I've been here.

[16] Y'all didn't choose Me. I cut you out of the herd for a job; that is to ride the trail doin' the good works that will last. If folks know Me 'cause of your work, you can ask things of the Father in My name and He'll do it.

[17-18] I'm still a-sayin' that to love one another is the first and foremost part. The works don't mean anything without that. And if the world hates ya, well, y'all need to know it hated Me first.

> Chapter 15 Just Thinkin
>
> Before barbed wire crisscrossed the plains, ranchers gathered up their herds in what was called a "general roundup". Cowboys would scour the countryside looking for cattle with the *brand* for their ranch. This was the only way they could identify which cattle belonged to them. It was the *brand* that identified them as their own. Jesus in the 15th chapter of John tells us that as a born-again child of God we bear identification as though *branded* by God the Father. That mark identifies us as belonging to Jesus. We can expect the unbelieving world under control of the enemy to treat us the same as it treated Him.

[19] See, y'all don't belong to this world anymore. If ya did, it would love ya like its own. But 'cause I called y'all out, this here world hates you for sure.

[20] Do y'all recollect what I done taught ya, 'A drover is not gonna fair better than his trail boss.' If they come after Me, they're gonna come after you too. If they heeded My word, then they'll heed yours.

Thinkin' Questions

1. In the verses above what is the main thing Jesus wants His followers to hold on to?

2. As true believers, how can we expect to be treated by the unbelieving world?

3. Is your brand visible? Does the world know you belong to God?

²¹ *"Things are gonna get mighty tough for y'all on account of My name. Ya see, other folks don't know the One who done sent Me.*

²² *If I hadn't come along and told folks about Myself, the ones who turned Me out would still be plumb ignorant. But now they've heard and still won't come away from their sin. They have no excuse, no-sir-ee.*

²³ *For sure, any fella or gal that hates Me hates My Father too. That just ain't right.*

²⁴ *Anyhow, if I had not done the miracles among 'em like no one else could, they wouldn't have the sin of rejectin' their own salvation. But they done witnessed these things and they hate Me for it and My Father too.*

²⁵ *They've done gone and fulfilled the Scripture written down in their own Law that prophesied, 'They hated Me for no good reason' (Psalm 35:19 and Psalm 69:4).*

²⁶ *When the Trail Guide comes, the Spirit of Truth who comes from the Father, He will ride along the trail with ya. I will be the One to send Him out and He will for sure be tellin' y'all the true things about Me,*

²⁷ *and y'all will be tellin' folks about Me too, on account you've been ridin' the trail with Me from the very start."*

> Everyone who hears the gospel of Jesus Christ has a choice of accepting or rejecting Him into their lives as Savior of their eternal souls. They have a choice to make whether or not to accept His pardon for sin as the only One who can save them for eternity.

Thinkin' Questions

1. What is the sin mentioned in **verse 24** that cannot be forgiven as one passes into eternity? **Read also Matthew 13:58; John 5:38-40; John 8:24; Acts 13:46; Mark 16:16; Hebrews 3:12.**

2. In **verse 26** what name is given for the Trail Guide as we ride to tell others the good news of Jesus Christ? _____ Other Scriptures identify Him further such as: **Mark 13:10-11; John 14:26; John 16:13; Acts 1:8.**

Chapter Sixteen

Rough Trail Ahead

[1] Jesus told 'em straight, "I have told you wranglers these things so you won't get tripped up.

[2] Y'all are gonna get plumb thrown out of the synagogues; but that won't be nothin'. The time will come when they'll come gunnin' for ya thinkin' they're doin' God a favor by killin' ya.

[3] Y'all can reckon they'll be doin' all this 'cause they don't know Me or the Father.

[4] I'm tellin' y'all this stuff so ya won't be scratchin' your heads about it when the time comes. It will come to your mind then that I done told ya. There weren't any need to let y'all know about all this trouble before now, seein' how I was with you and all.

[5] But now, I'll be headin' on back up yonder to the One who sent Me and it don't seem like even one of you fellas wants to know just where it is I'm goin'.

[6] Ever since I said I'd be ridin' out, I reckon' you fellas are feelin' so sorrowful that ya just ain't thought it through.

[7] But fact is, it's to y'all's benefit for Me to ride on out; on account if I don't get along, the Trail Guide won't come. But if I ride away, I will send Him along to ya.

[8] And from the minute He rides in, He'll be persuadin' folks of the world in regards to what's right and wrong, and the judgment,

[9] and the deadly sin situation folks are in if they don't believe in Me.

[10] And on account I'm goin' back to the Father, the Trail Guide will be the One to show ya what's right.

[11] And He'll be warnin' folks about the judgment 'cause the ol' devil and his evil control over this world has done already been judged."

Thinkin' Questions

1. According to the Scriptures above, what are some of the purposes of the new Trail Guide (Holy Spirit) in relation to the world.

_____

_____

_____

_____

_____

[12] *"I have a heap more stuff to tell y'all, but ya wouldn't be able to take it all in just yet.*

[13-15] *But when the Trail Guide comes, He will lead you rightly into all the truth. Ya see, He won't be speakin' out of His own notions, no-sir-ee. He will tell y'all only what He hears. And He will let y'all in on some things that's gonna happen on up the trail. For sure, He will be givin' the glory to Me while He's lookin' out for ya. He'll be takin' things of Mine and passin' them along to you. Ya see, everything the Father has is Mine too. It's on account of that I can say He will be passin' those things along from Me to you.*

[16] *I'm tellin' ya the time's a-comin' real soon when y'all won't see Me for a spell. Then after a bit you will see Me again."*

[17-18] *Jesus' pardners were wonderin' and scratchin' their heads again over all this. Some of the fellas were sayin', "What in the world is He talkin' about? We ain't gonna see Him . . . then after a spell we'll see Him 'cause He's goin' to the Father?" Some fellas asked, "So what's He mean by 'after a bit'? How long is He talkin'? We don't get it."*

[19] *Jesus knew what was goin' on in their heads, so He said to 'em: "Y'all are gettin' all hung up on Me sayin', 'y'all won't see Me for a spell; and in a little while you will see Me again.'*

[20] *Come on, I want y'all to understand that some powerful grief is about to come your way that will have y'all cryin' in the dust. And though y'all will be despairin', the world all around will be celebratin'. But your sorrowin' will be turned to pure grinnin' after a short spell.*

[21] *It's like when labor comes on a woman at the time to give birth. It brings powerful sufferin', but after she has the child, she forgets about her pain on account she's so happy that her young'un has safely gotten born."*

Thinkin' Questions

1. In **verses 13-15** above, how much of what the Father has belongs to the Son, and who has the authority to pass those things along to us?

2. What great Biblical concept is indicated in **verses 13-15** regarding the Father, Son, and Holy Spirit? _____. **Read Matthew 28:18-20** and understand in whose name we are to make disciples.

   Other Scripture passages also allude to the reality of the Trinity, the Three-In-One God. Among them are: **Genesis 1:26** --God references Himself with a plural term. In **John 1:1-3**, Who is in the beginning with God? _____.

   In **2 Samuel 23:2-3** David speaks of all three persons of the _____ as the _____ of the Lord, the _____ of Israel and the _____ Who rules over men justly.

²² "I can see this is plumb tearin' y'all up; but I give you My word, I will see you again, and y'all will be so proud to see Me, no one will ever take that joy outta your hearts.

²³ Then, y'all will get it figured out and ya won't be scratchin' your heads and wonderin' about all these things. Truth is if you ask the Father for anything in My name, He will give it to you. He will help ya understand.

²⁴ Up 'til now, y'all haven't asked for anything in My name. But I'm tellin' ya, 'Ask and you will receive, so you can be fully blessed.'

²⁵ I've explained all these things in figurative words. But a time's comin' when I won't speak that way any longer; but with plain words I will tell y'all about the Father.

²⁶ In that day y'all can ask things in My name. That's not sayin' I will be askin' the Father on your behalf. There won't be need for that; no, you'll be askin' Him yourself.

²⁷⁻²⁸ For ya see, the Father loves you. He's mighty proud 'cause you love Me and believe that I came along from Him. When I rode into the world, I came from the Father; and now I'm ridin' out and goin' back to the Father."

²⁹⁻³⁰ His pardners said to Him, "Okay now, You're talkin' plain to us. We're hearin' what You're sayin'. We surely do believe that You know all things; no need for any of us wranglers to question it. On account of that we believe You came from God for sure."

³¹⁻³² Jesus answered, "So now you do believe? I tell you a time is comin' up fast. In fact it's already here; a time when y'all are gonna scatter. You're all gonna hightail it home like a bunch of newborn calves and leave Me alone. But I am not alone because the Father is with Me.

³³ I've told y'all what's comin' up the trail so you can have some real peace in Me knowin' how it is. In the world you will have lots of trouble. But have courage, I have overcome the world."

Chapter 16   Just Thinkin

There is an old saying, "Still water runs deep." I've not met many honest-to-goodness cowboys that use a lot of unnecessary words when they speak. My cowboy grandfather was like that. He didn't talk much but what he said was worth listening to. His words came from a deep pool of wisdom. Folks were amazed when they heard Jesus speak. It was said by some, "He *teaches* as one having authority, and not as the scribes" (Matthew 7:29). John records that near the end of His ministry Jesus spoke to His disciples not in figures of speech but clearly and directly. Soon He would be leaving them and another 'Helper' the Holy Spirit would come and He would remind them of all that He taught them. *"But when the Trail Guide comes, He will lead you rightly into all the truth . . . For sure, He will be givin' the glory to Me while He's lookin' out for ya. He'll be takin' the things of Mine and passin' them along to you."* John 16:13-14

Thinkin' Question

1. It is fairly evident that Jesus' pardners did not fully comprehend what He was saying to them. However, they are putting their trust in Him and telling us what they did believe at that particular time. **Verse 30** reveals two statements of faith from Jesus' pardners. List them here:

   1.

   2.

Chapter Seventeen

Talkin' to His Pa

In **John 17** John jots down a deeply personal conversation between Jesus and His Father. Actually it is a prayer, the longest of Jesus' recorded prayers in scripture. Some key elements stand out; one being that Jesus defines eternal life as that of knowing God the Father and His Son through an everlasting personal relationship. In verses 2-3 Jesus acknowledges that His Father has given Him authority to give eternal life to all who belong to Him –those whom the Father has given Him. He makes it clear that knowing the only true God comes through knowing His Son Jesus Christ. This is indeed our salvation for which He was sent.

Notice a couple of things Jesus acknowledges about those who believe in Him: One, they were given to Him from the Father because they believed that He was sent by the Father and trusted in His Word. *"I have done made Your name known to all the folks livin' here on earth who You surely gave Me. From the start they had a heart for You, and You done give 'em over to Me, and they've been trustin' Your word"* (John 17:6).

Secondly, He acknowledges to His Father that of all those given to Him, He lost none of them who had truly chosen Him. Judas Iscariot was not one of them. Apparently each disciple reached a point of decision to receive Christ. Judas chose rather to exploit Him. *"For the time I was with these fellas after You give 'em to Me, I looked out after 'em to see no harm came to any one of 'em. In Your name I kept these pardners close and there didn't anything happen to a one, 'cept that one who chose in himself to turn bad, like was prophesied in the Scripture"* (John 17:12).

Another key element is that Jesus asks the Father to keep His followers safe and secure in His eternal power— *"I'm not askin' that You take 'em out of this world, but to keep 'em from the evil one"* (John 17:15). Safety of our souls is secure in Jesus Christ. Once we belong to Him we can't be lost (John 10:28-30). As the Apostle Paul wrote *"Nothing can separate us from the love of Christ."* Romans 8:35-39

It is important to understand that Jesus' prayer is for all believers through all the ages, even for those of us who are living now and those who will come after us— *"I'm not just askin' Your favor for these fellas and gals I have now, but for all the ones comin' along up the trail who will believe in Me on account of them"* (John 17:20).

Finally Jesus prays for unity in verse 21-23. He speaks about the unity that He and the Father have. He prays that believers may also be bound together as one in a way that shows God's love to the world. To be successful, team ropers must work together in unity. Each has a different function; one to head, the other to heel, but both work together each dependent upon the other to complete the task. So it is in the Church. Each member has different gifts and functions but each works together in unity to fulfill the purpose of bringing honor and Glory to God the Father through the Church. Unbelievers will take notice of such a group of believers.

Chapter Seventeen – Talkin' to His Pa

[1] After Jesus got through tellin' His pardners straight how it was gonna be, He raised up His eyes toward heaven and started some serious prayin', *"Howdy Pa, I reckon it's about time for this thing to get on. I'm askin' for You to give honor and glory to Your Son so Your Son can give honor and glory back to You.*

[2-3] *You gave Him genuine authority over all that is flesh, so that He can give life of the everlastin' kind to them You done give Him. The everlastin' kind of life bein' such that any fella or gal can rightly know You, the one and only true God, and Your Son Jesus Christ who You sent into this world.*

[4] *I done glorified You on this here earth by gettin' done what You rightly give Me to do.*

[5] *So Father, I'm askin' here and now for You to glorify Me with the same glory We had together 'fore the world even was.*

[6-7] *I have done made Your name known to all the folks livin' here on earth who You surely gave Me. From the start they had a heart for You, and You done give 'em over to Me, and they've been trustin' Your word. Now they rightly know that everything I have came straight from You;*

[8] *Ya see, they have taken and believed the words You done give Me to speak out to 'em and now they reckon I came from You and that You sent Me.*

[9] *So I'm askin' some things, Pa, on behalf of the ones You have done give Me, on account of they are Yours. I'm not askin' on behalf of the world of folks that want to turn Me out, but for them in Your own outfit.*

[10] *I know all the things that I have are Yours and what's Yours is Mine, and I have been plumb glorified on account of that.*

[11] *I'm about to come on home. I won't be in this world any longer but the rest of 'em have to stay on here. Almighty Father be a-keepin' watch over them by the power that's in Your name, the name You gave Me; so they'll be one, same as You and Me.*

[12] *For the time I was with these fellas after You give 'em to Me, I looked out after 'em to see no harm came to any one of 'em. In Your name I kept these pardners close and there didn't anything happen to a one, 'cept that one who chose in himself to turn bad, like was prophesied in the Scripture.*

[13] *I'm comin' to You now, and I'm askin' these things while I am still in the world so they can be filled up with this joy of Mine.*

[14] *I done passed along to 'em all You told Me, and the world hates 'em on account of it. They don't belong in this world any more than I do.*

[15-16] I'm not askin' that You take 'em out of this world, but to keep 'em from the evil one. They're not part of this world just like I'm not part of it, no Sir.

[17-18] Father keep 'em strong, rightly cut out for Yourself. Let the truth of Your word be makin' their hearts pure and keepin' 'em cleaned up. I'm a sendin' them out into the world to work, same as You sent Me.

[19] It's on their account I keep Myself clean and set apart for You by the truth; so they also can be made pure and strong, set apart for Me by the truth.

[20] I'm not just askin' Your favor for these fellas and gals I have now, but for all the ones comin' along up the trail who will believe in Me on account of them.

[21-22] I'm askin' for all the ones who believe to be bound together and braided into one, like a good rope. You are in Me, Pa, and I am in You. Let them be in Us makin' it so the world can believe You sent Me. I have done given them glory, same as You gave Me, so they can be one together just like You and I are one.

[23] When the world sees the folks who believe in Me livin' in harmony 'cause I am in them and You are in Me; well, then I 'xpect they will reckon You sent Me for sure and You love them like You loved Me.

[24] Pa, I have a real hankerin' to have everyone in My outfit ridin' with Me up yonder in all My glory. I reckon I want 'em especially to know the love between You and Me since before this here world got started.

[25-26] Oh Good Father, even though the folks in the world, for the most part, just never got rightly acquainted with Ya. I've always known You and now I reckon these know that You done sent Me. Ya see, I've done give 'em a real good picture of who You are, and I will keep on doing that very thing, so Your same love what showed up in Me, will make a home in their hearts right along with Myself.

Thinkin' Question

1. In **chapter 17**, Jesus prays for His followers for all time. List some things Jesus asked the Father regarding you personally and the body of believers as a whole. _____

   _____

   _____

   _____

   _____

Chapter Eighteen

Stabbed in the Back

Chapter Eighteen – Stabbed in the Back

¹ After Jesus was done prayin' to His Father, He and His pardners rode out across the Kidron Valley and made their way up to a certain place where there was a grove of trees.

² Judas Iscariot was out doin' his dirty work. He figured Jesus would be headed to one of His favorite spots to pray after supper. Jesus brought His pardners there fairly regular like.

³ So here come Judas with a posse of Roman soldiers and their cohorts. Along with 'em was some religious so-called officers sent by the chief priests and for sure some of them big shot Pharisees with their lanterns and torches. And you bet your boots there was plenty of weapons among 'em. It was quite a site approachin' in the dark of night.

Chapter 18 Just Thinkin
The "grove of trees" mentioned in verse 1 was at the Mount of Olives in an area known as the Garden of Gethsemane. For a full account of Jesus' time there before the mob arrived, refer to Matthew 26:36-46 and Luke 22:41-44.

⁴⁻⁶ But ya see, Jesus knew all along what was takin' place so He went out to meet 'em face to face and asked, *"Who are y'all lookin' for?"* "Jesus the Nazarene", they announced all high and mighty like. Jesus done spoke right up sayin', *"I am He"*. For sure that no good Judas was standin' right up in the front with 'em.

⁶ But Jesus' words were so powerful when He said, *"I am He,"* the whole herd of 'em fell backwards stunned to the ground.

⁷⁻⁸ So Jesus started over. He asked again, *"Who is it y'all are lookin' for?"* They answered real gentle-like this time, "Jesus the Nazarene". Jesus answered 'em, *"I done told y'all who I am; so, if I'm the one y'all want, let these other men here be on their way."*

⁹ Jesus said that 'cause He had done give His word earlier to the Father, *"Of all those You gave Me, I didn't lose any of 'em; no-sir-ee, not even one."*

Thinkin' Questions

1. In the scene described, why did the men seeking Jesus fall to the ground stunned when He spoke in **verse 6? Read Psalms 33:6-10 & John 8:23-24.**

2. When the mob came to arrest Jesus, He went out to meet them. Regardless of appearances, who was in control in **verses 3-8** above? _____ **Review Jesus' statement in John 10:17-18.**

3. What can we learn from the way Jesus meets the worst of trouble face to face?

4. What was the driving force behind the actions of Judas and the religious leaders who opposed Jesus? **Review John 8:44 & Luke 22:53; also Ephesians 6:12.**

¹⁰⁻¹¹ Well now Peter was carryin' a weapon of his own. Figurin' Jesus was in desperate trouble, he drew out a blade and swung it, cuttin' the right ear of the chief priest's slave plumb off. The fella's name was Malchus. But Jesus said, *"Put your knife away, Peter. This cup that the Father done give Me, I'm gonna drink it."*

¹²⁻¹⁴ So Jesus let them Roman soldiers and their generals and the Jewish officers arrest Him, and He let 'em tie Him up, too. And so they hauled Jesus away first to the old high priest, Annas. He was the father-in-law of Caiaphas who was the high priest now, ya see. Guess ol' Annas wanted in on the deal somehow. Caiaphas, the high priest, was the one who prophesied to the Jewish leaders that he reckoned it was better for one person to die for the people.

¹⁵⁻¹⁶ Now Peter was trailin' after Jesus and so was another pardner. Since the high priest was acquainted with the other pardner, they let him enter into the high priest's court with Jesus. Peter was left standin' outside the gate. So the pardner who was let in went out and spoke a word to the gatekeeper and brought Peter on in to the courtyard.

¹⁷⁻¹⁸ The one a-tendin' the gate was a servant girl. She blabbered out to Peter, "Hey, ain't you one of the pardners of the Man they done arrested?" Peter said, "No, I am not!" Now there was some other hands out there and some officers a-warmin' themselves by a campfire 'cause it had gotten mighty cold. So Peter joined 'em tryin' to lay low.

Thinkin' Questions

To capture a more complete picture of the scene surrounding the arrest of Jesus, refer to other gospel accounts: **Matthew 26:47-58; Luke 22:47-53.**

1. Why do you think there are variations in testimonies of those who were there?

2. Luke was a physician. What information does he include about the slave who had his ear cut off? **Luke 22:49-53**

3. Name some characteristics of Jesus that come through in all the eyewitness accounts? **Choose from the list in Galatians 5:22-23.**

[19] The old high priest was questionin' Jesus about His pardners and about what He had been teachin', and he was makin' plenty of accusations and insinuations, yes-sir-ee.

[20-21] Jesus told him, *"I've always spoke out in the open in front of everybody. I've been teachin' in synagogues and in the temple, any place where Jewish folks naturally get together. Anybody can come. I've got nothin' to hide. Why are you questionin' Me for? There's plenty of folks who've heard My teachin'. They know what I said. Ask them."*

[22] There was a hot-shot religious officer standin' close by, and he didn't like it none what Jesus was sayin'. He busted Jesus one in the mouth and snarled, "Is that how You answer the high priest?"

[23] Jesus said to the officer, *"If I have said somethin' that's not the truth, then tell folks what I said that was wrong. But If I spoke the rightful truth, then why did you hit Me?"*

[24] Old Annas had done heard enough. He sent Jesus, still tied up, off to Caiaphas, the high priest.

[25] Now Peter was still standin' out there by the campfire warmin' hisself. Some of those fellas started doggin' him, "Hey, ain't you one of His pardners, too?" Peter denied it and said, "No way, I ain't."

[26] One of the servants of the high priest who happened to be there was a relative of the fella whose ear Peter cut off. He recognized him and popped off, "Didn't I see you there in the garden with Him?"

[27] Peter swore and sure 'nough for the third time denied ever knowin' Jesus. And then a rooster crowed loud and clear just like Jesus said.

~⚬══════⚬~

Thinkin' Questions

1. Remember, Peter was *there* in the courtyard. Most of the other disciples were hiding. Did Peter's denial make him a failure as a Christian? Explain.

2. What did Peter learn about himself through his experience in the courtyard? How did it make him better qualified to lead other believers?

3. Have you ever experienced a time of testing and felt like you failed only to eventually realize that it was the failure that made you stronger? _____ Spend some time reflecting on these experiences and thank God for what He accomplished in your heart through those times.

28 After more of the same with Caiaphas, Jesus permitted 'em to wrangle Him over to the judgment hall at the governor's place. This nonsense had been goin' on all night long; so it was now early the next mornin',

the day of Passover. Now them religious know-it-alls with their rules would make themselves unclean if they went in there to see the governor, so they had to wait outside. They sure didn't want to miss eatin' at the big feast. Ya see, enterin' a non-Jewish place like that would have been against their law.

29 So ol' Governor Pilate came out to the Jews and said, "Okay, what charges are y'all bringin' against this Man? This better be good."

30 Then those high and mighty religious chiefs said, "If this Man weren't the worst of criminals, we wouldn't have brung Him to ya."

31 Pilate snorted, "Is that right? Well, y'all take Him and judge Him yourselves by your own law. What are y'all pesterin' me for?" So those Jewish honchos actin' all dignified said, "It's because our law doesn't permit us to put anyone to death."

32 Yep, it would sure 'nough be just like Jesus said about how He was gonna die. He had done seen it all comin'.

> Chapter 18   **ঙ৩৫৪**   Just Thinkin'
>
> In the latter part of the 19th century, Judge Roy Bean served as Justice of Peace in Val Verde County, Texas. He called himself "The Law West of the Pecos." He held court in a saloon along the Rio Grande in a desolate stretch of the Chihuahua Desert of Southwest Texas. Though not a trained lawyer or a genuine judge, Bean held court, pronounced verdicts, and handed down sentences, even sentences to be hanged to death. His word was final and he never allowed hung juries or appeals. He was nicknamed the "Hanging Judge." After Jesus was arrested He was brought before Annas, and much like Judge Bean's court, it was an illegal trial. There were no witnesses as Jewish law required, so they hired false witnesses (Matthew 26:60-61). The trials of Jesus were brutal. Imagine a prisoner in chains being struck and mocked during a trial as Jesus was (John 18:22 & Mark 14:65). Jesus withstood the trials and beatings that fateful night and was ultimately nailed to a cross to suffer and die for us that we might have life!
>
> **ঙ৩৫৪**

Thinkin' Questions

1. What prophecy was Jesus fulfilling by permitting the religious leaders to accuse and condemn Him? Why did He not defend Himself? **Read Luke 22:37 & 52-54; also Mark 14:48-49. Review also Isaiah 53:4-8.**

2. Did Jesus know just how His arrest and trials would play out? _____ Review the words of Jesus in **John 12:32-33. Also read Matthew 17:9; Matthew 20:18-19; Mark 9:31 and Luke 9:22.** How much did He know?

[33-34] So Pilate went back to the judgment hall with the charges and sent a deputy to fetch Jesus. Pilate asked Jesus straight out, "Are You the King of the Jews?" Jesus answered him, *"Are you askin' Me this 'cause of your own ponderin', or is it on account of what somebody's been' tellin' you about Me?"*

[35] Then ol' Pilate said to Him, "I ain't no Jew, am I? It was Your own people, the chief priests who dragged You up here to me. So what thing did You do to get them all so riled up?"

[36] Jesus just told him, *"My kingdom is not of this world. If My kingdom were here in this world I would've let My pardners defend Me; and I would not have let the Jews arrest Me. No, My kingdom is not part of this here earthly domain."*

[37] When Pilate heard that he said, "So You are a king?" Jesus said, *"You are plumb right about that--I am a king. The very reason I was born and came into this world was so I could tell people the truth and show 'em what is right. Everyone who loves truth listens to what I say."*

[38] Pilate said, "What is truth?" And he threw up his hands and went back out to where the Jews were. He declared to the lot of 'em, "This man ain't committed no crime. I can't find one thing He's done wrong."

[39] Pilate went on sayin', "Here's how y'all can get out of this mess: A tradition of you Jews is such that every year at Passover, I let one of your outlaws outta jail. Do y'all want me to let the King of the Jews go free?"

[40] But then the mob of Jews started carryin' on somethin' awful and whined, "No, don't let this Man go, but let Barabbas out of jail." Now this Barabbas fella was nothin' but a no good robber and an outlaw.

Thinkin' Questions

1. In **verses 36-37** above, Jesus tells Pilate that He is not from this world. According to **John 3:13-14** where did Jesus come from and what was the purpose of His coming?

2. The response of the mob in **verse 40** is hard to understand. Only one thing would make human beings act so violently against the Son of God. Jesus explains it back in **John 8:44-47** when He was talking to the religious leaders. What sad truth is revealed by this mob's actions?

Chapter Nineteen

The Cross

¹ So it happened, Pilate for no reason at all had Jesus whipped tryin' to please them bloodthirsty skunks. It was a mighty sad state of affairs.

²⁻³ After the whippin' was done, the soldiers twisted up a crown made out of thorn bushes and shoved it down on the brow of Jesus' head. Then they come up with a purple robe to put on Him. And they was just gettin' wound up. They had a great ol' time mockin' Him. They were punchin' and hittin' Jesus in the face and sayin' to Him, "Hail, King of the Jews!"

⁴ Then Pilate went out again and sent for Jesus. He said to the Jews, "Look, I'm bringin' Him back to y'all whipped near to death and I still don't find no reason to bring charges against Him. We're done."

⁵ When the deputies showed up with Jesus wearin' the crown of thorns and that purple robe, Pilate said to them, "Look, here's your Man!"

⁶ But when the chief priests and the Jewish officers saw Him they started in hollerin', "Crucify! Crucify!" Pilate was dumbfounded. He said, "Y'all take Him and crucify Him yourselves; I don't find no wrong in Him."

⁷ But the Jews yelled back, "We have a law that plainly says He has to die 'cause He claims that He is the Son of God!"

⁸ That got ol' Pilate plumb scared. He didn't want no part of killin' the Son of God.

⁹ He went back inside the judgment hall and asked Jesus, "Just where did You come from?" But Jesus had nothin' to say. --He was lettin' this all play out.

Thinkin' Questions

1. Hate, like that demonstrated by this murderous mob, grows out of sin hidden deep in a person's spirit. As Jesus encountered sins of the flesh in people's lives, He responded with compassion and mercy for those enslaved to sin. How was Jesus' approach different toward pride, arrogance and self-righteousness (sins of the spirit). In which category would you put yourself? **Read Luke 7:36-50; Luke 11:43-44; Luke 18:10-14; Matthew 23:13-14 & 23-28.**

2. Have you asked God to forgive *all* of your sins through the blood of Jesus Christ? **Read John 3:16; Romans 5:6-11; Romans 8:1-2 and 1 John 1:9.**

[10] Pilate got plumb exasperated then and said, "You are not talkin' to me? Don't You know that I'm the one who has the authority to say if You live or die today? I have the power to let You go free or crucify You!"

[11] Jesus answered him, *"You don't have any authority over Me except that which was done given you from above. Ya see, that's why the one who handed Me over to you has the sin that's worse than yours."*

[12] Pilate plumb tried about everything to release Him, but them Jews kept shoutin', "If you let this Man go, then you ain't no friend of Caesar. Anyone that makes himself out to be a king is against Caesar."

[13] That put Pilate in a predicament for sure. Caesar could have his head. Then he brought Jesus out and sat down on the judgment seat where he would sure 'nough make his final decision.

[14] It was now high noon on the very day they was gettin' ready for the Passover. It was supposed to start at sundown. Pilate then said to the Jews, "Behold, your King!"

[15] That got 'em riled up more than ever. "Take Him out and crucify Him!" they hollered over and over. Plate asked 'em, "Are you sayin' you want me to crucify your King?" The chief priests clenched it then. They said, "The only king we have is Caesar."

[16] So Pilate right then and there handed Jesus over to be crucified.

Thinkin' Questions

1. Jesus made an interesting statement about Pilate's authority. What does the Bible say about authority of rulers? **Read Proverbs 8:15-16; Romans 13:1; also 1 Peter 2:13-17.**

2. What if a ruler becomes evil or abuses his power? **Read Proverbs 29:2; Jeremiah 51:23-24.**

3. In the end, Who is the ultimate authority? **Matthew 28:18; Philippians 2:9-11; 1 Corinthians 15:24-26; Revelation 17:14 and Revelation 19:11-16.**

¹⁷ The Roman soldiers took Jesus and they made Him carry His own cross through town. Jesus let them push Him on up the trail to a place called "The Place of a Skull." Some folks know it by its Hebrew name, "Golgotha".

¹⁸ When they got there, they nailed Jesus to a dirty old cross. There were two other men crucified with Jesus at the same time, one on each side; Jesus was in the middle.

¹⁹⁻²⁰ Pilate had 'em put up a sign on that ol' cross that read, "JESUS THE NAZARENE, THE KING OF THE JEWS." The sign was written in Hebrew, Latin, and Greek so most everybody could read it. Lots of Jews were a-comin' and goin' from the city; plenty of folks seen it for sure.

²¹ I reckon the chief priests of the Jews were about to choke on what that sign said, 'cause they went to Pilate and demanded, "Don't write 'The King of the Jews' on His cross but make it read 'He said, I am King of the Jews.'"

²² Well ol' Pilate told 'em straight out, "I ain't changin' what I wrote."

²³ While Jesus was hangin' there on the cross, the soldiers who had nailed Him tore up His robe, dividin' it into four parts for each one to have an equal share. Then they took His shirt He wore under His robe. It didn't have no seams in it bein' it was made of one piece of cloth.

²⁴ So they decided rather than tearin' it up they would throw dice for it to see who would take it. Now that very thing had done been prophesied a long time back in the Scriptures sayin': "They divided My outer garments among them and for My clothing they cast lots" (Psalm 22:18).

²⁵ Them soldiers did this thing whilst Jesus' mother, Mary, and her sister who was another Mary, and Mary Magdalene were all standin' right near the cross.

²⁶ Jesus looked out and saw His mama there with the pardner who He was mighty fond of standin' close by her. He said to His mother, *"Dear woman, here now is your son!"*

²⁷ And He said to His pardner, *"Here now is your mother!"* From then on that pardner took care of her like she was his own kin.

Thinkin' Questions

1. By our sinful natures and God given free will, both the Jews and the Romans, --indeed all of us, fulfilled the prophecies surrounding the death of Jesus down to the last detail. **Read a portion of Peter's sermon in Acts 2:36-39. Write in your own words, your prayer of confession to the Lord Jesus Christ.** _____

   _____

   _____

   _____

Notes

²⁸ Now Jesus knowin' that everything had done been carried out spoke up sayin', *"I'm thirsty!"* This was so it would fully measure up to what was wrote down in the Good Book. (Psalm 22:15)

²⁹ Ya see, they did just like the Scriptures had said, they soaked up a sponge with sour vinegar and lifted it up to Jesus' mouth on a hyssop branch. (Psalm 69:21)

³⁰ When Jesus had done tasted the sour vinegar He said, *"It is finished!"* And He bowed His head and died.

³¹ The Jews were frettin' now 'cause the Passover Sabbath was about to commence in a few hours. They convinced Pilate to have the criminals' legs broke so they would go ahead and die and the bodies could be taken down. That way it wouldn't spoil their Passover Sabbath day.

³²⁻³³ The soldiers came and broke the legs of the other two men who had done been crucified with Jesus. But when they came to Jesus they saw He had done already died, so they didn't need to break His legs.

³⁴ But one of the soldiers went up and thrust his spear into Jesus' side. Blood and water came pourin' out. That right there was sure proof Jesus was dead.

³⁵ The one who done witnessed every bit of this is tellin' it just like it happened. And his account is the solemn truth. He knows without a doubt that he's tellin' the truth so y'all can believe.

Chapter 19   ℰↃ◯ℛ   Just Thinkin

On our little ranch, there was always work to be done so my father would assign chores for me to do, like feed the cattle, repair a broken fence, dig up prickly pear plants out of the pasture, clean the stalls, and whatever else he could think of. Later he would always ask me, "Son, did you get it all done?" And I'd usually say, "Yep, I finished the work you gave me to do." Jesus came to earth, sent by His Father to perform an assignment He had given Him. That assignment involved being nailed to a cross to die as our perfect substitute in order that our sins may be forgiven. The last words Jesus spoke from the cross before giving up His life in death were addressed to His Father, *"It is finished!"* "It is over . . . the task is complete, the work You sent Me to do is done!" The death of the Son of God was once and for all. Nothing else, no other work, no other sacrifice will ever have to be paid for our salvation. His death on the cross finished the work His Father gave Him to do!

ℰↃ◯ℛ

Thinkin' Questions

1. Read the following Scriptures and try to explain in your own words why Jesus had to die: **Genesis 2:15-17 and 3:1-24; Romans 5:10-12 & 15; Romans 8:1-4.** List other Scriptures that help you explain God's plan of salvation for mankind.

2. In our pride, the concept of a substitute to suffer the penalty of our own sin and guilt is difficult to accept. We want to pay our own way. What does Scripture have to say about the substitutionary death of Jesus Christ? **Read Isaiah 53:4-6; Romans 3:23-26; 2 Corinthians 5:17-19 & 21. Also read 1 Peter 2:24-25 & 3:18 and 1 John 2:1-2 & 4:10.**

[36] So here was another thing that come about and fulfilled what Scripture done told beforehand, "Not a bone of Him shall be broken" (Psalm 34:20).

[37] And in another place it says, "They shall look on Him whom they pierced" (Zechariah 12:10).

[38] It was gettin' late in the day when a fella named Joseph of Arimathea come to ask Pilate for the body of Jesus. Seems Joseph, a well respected man, was a secret follower. He had done believed Jesus and was plumb obliged to Him, but he was afraid the Jewish leaders would ruin him. Pilate was agreeable and so Joseph took Jesus' body away for burial.

[39] Another fella, ol' Nicodemus, had come along to help. He was the fella who came to visit with Jesus at night on account of his position and all. Nicodemus had brought with him about a hundred pounds of spices—a mix of myrrh and other stuff.

[40] So they took the body of Jesus and wrapped it up real tight in strips of linen cloth along with the spices; 'cause ya see that was the right and proper way the Jews buried people in those days.

[41] Now there was a garden close by where they buried the dead in tombs. It weren't too far from the place where Jesus was crucified. There was a brand new tomb there, never been used.

[42] After they had finished preparin' Jesus' body, the sun was settin' and it was time for the Passover Sabbath to begin. So since the tomb was close by, they laid Jesus' body to rest in that place.

> Other scriptures note that Joseph of Arimathea closed up the tomb as was customary in those days by lettin' a big stone roll down into place over the entrance. (Matthew 27:60, Mark 15:46)

Thinkin' Questions

1. Jesus was Jewish and kept the customs of His day even in death. Joseph of Arimathea and Nicodemus would be known for their devotion to Jesus since their selfless act would be a part of public record. They kept their faith a secret up until now thus maintaining their position. God's plan included that they would fulfill the burial, thus proclaiming their faith. What does God's word say about someone who will NEVER acknowledge Jesus publicly? Is that possible for a true believer? **See Luke 11:33; Matthew 10-32-33; Luke 12:8-9.**

2. The death of a loved one or friend brings sorrow, grief and mourning. Things may seem hopeless and bleak. Burial seems final, as it did for Jesus' followers. According to the promise of Jesus, Who will comfort us during these times of sorrow? **Review – John 14:26-27 and John 16:6-7.**

Chapter Twenty

The Grave Couldn't Hold Him

Chapter 20 — Just Thinkin

Was the resurrection of Jesus real? You bet your boots it was! There were some then and many since who have tried to make it not so, claiming that it was a hoax or just a story that the disciples made up. But the truth is, the resurrection of Jesus has withstood the test of time. As believers we still look back to that empty tomb and rejoice that death could not hold the Son of God. He is risen . . . He is risen indeed! "He is not here, for He has risen, just as He said. . ." (Matthew 28:6a).

1 (Now Jesus had been buried and the tomb done sealed on Friday 'round sundown on account that's when the Sabbath started.) Early Sunday mornin' before the sun came up, Mary Magdalene went out to the cemetery and found the big stone plumb taken away from the tomb.

2 So she ran away cryin' and upset lookin' for help. She found Peter and the other young pardner Jesus was so fond of and told 'em, "They've done taken the Lord out of the tomb and we don't know where they took Him or what they've done with Him!"

3-5 So Peter and the other pardner lit out runnin' fast as they could scramble to the tomb. They started out together but the younger pardner out ran Peter and got there first; and stoopin' down so he could see inside, he saw the strips of linen cloth just lyin' there still in their place in the tomb. He froze.

6-7 Peter was comin' up fast behind him and when he got there he just kept a-goin', bustin' right on into that tomb; and there he saw the strips of linen cloth lain just right. Right away he noticed the cloth that was wrapped around Jesus' head weren't with the other strips of cloth. It was done rolled up and laid off by itself.

8-10 After Peter went in, the other pardner who got there first stepped in too. Then he saw and believed that Jesus' body was gone. Ya see, they didn't yet understand the things in the Good Book about all this. Accordin' to the Scriptures, Jesus had to rise up from the dead. Jesus hadn't been able to get that across to 'em. So they just went on back to the house.

Thinkin' Questions

1. Now the rest of God's plan unfolds. We can rejoice that the story of Jesus does not end with His burial. Paul also proclaims the resurrection of Jesus in a sermon in **Acts 13:30-41.** He reminds us what the resurrection of Jesus actually means for us personally. **What is this good news stated in Acts 13:38?**

2. Jesus told the disciples beforehand that He would be killed and then rise from the dead. **Read Matthew 20:17-19; Mark 9:31-32; Mark 10:33-34; Luke 18:31-34.** Why do you think they didn't get it?

[11] But Mary stayed put right there standin' outside the tomb a-cryin' her heart out. Now while she was still cryin' she bent down and took a look inside the tomb.

[12-13] Well, lo 'n behold, there were two angels all dressed in white, sittin' one at the head and the other at the feet where Jesus' body had been. And they said to her, "Why are you cryin', miss?" And she said, "Because they have took my Lord, and I don't know where they've laid Him."

[14] Then, she turned around and saw Jesus standin' there, but she didn't know it was Jesus. She plumb didn't recognize Him.

[15] Jesus said to her, *"My dear woman, why are you cryin' so? Who are you looking for?"* Supposin' Him to be the gardener, Mary sobbed out, "Mister, if you've taken Him, tell me where He is, so I can go and get Him."

[16] But Jesus said to her, *"Mary!"* And when she heard Him speak her name, she knew who He was. She turned to Him and said, "Rabboni!" (That's Hebrew for Teacher).

[17] Jesus said to her, *"Whoa now. Ya can't hold on to Me just yet 'cause first I gotta go up to see My Pa. But go on now to My pardners and tell 'em this: 'I am goin' up to My Father and your Father, and to My God and your God.'"*

[18] So Mary Magdalene ran straight in on the pardners plenty excited, a-makin' the announcement, "I have seen the Lord!" Then she told 'em everything He had told her.

[19] On that same Sunday evenin' the pardners were hidin' out all together behind locked doors 'cause they were plumb scared the Jewish leaders might come after them next. All of a sudden there was Jesus standin' right in the middle of the room. He said to the fellas, *"Howdy pardners, peace be with ya now."*

[20] Then He showed 'em His hands and His side. Well, the pardners were tickled to death to see the Lord. That changed everything!

Thinkin' Questions

1. What does the Bible say about the disciples reaction to Mary Magdalene's news? **Read Luke 24:9-12; Mark 16:9-11.**

2. What truth changed the disciples from hopelessness to faith and how does that knowledge affect believers today? **Review John 11:25-26.**

3. What is the promise concerning our own resurrection? **1 Thessalonians 4:16-18**

²¹⁻²² And so Jesus said to them again, *"Peace be with you; like My Pa done sent Me, I am sendin' y'all, too."* Then He blessed 'em by breathin' on 'em sayin', *"Receive the Holy Spirit."*

²³ He made 'em His pardners all over again and told 'em, *"If you forgive anybody's sins, their sins are forgiven; but if you don't forgive their sins, they won't be forgiven."*

²⁴ But it so happened that one of the twelve pardners, Thomas, also known as the twin, weren't there when Jesus showed up.

²⁵ So the others were sayin' to Thomas, "We've done seen the Lord!" But Thomas wouldn't believe it. "Nope," he said, "I ain't gonna believe 'til I can see Him with the nail marks in His hands and put my finger where the nails were. And only if I can put my hand in His side and feel for myself where the spear went in, or else, I ain't gonna swallow it."

²⁶ The very next week the pardners were all together again inside with the doors locked again. Ol' Thomas was there this time. Jesus came again just standin' right in the middle of 'em sayin', *"Peace be with you."*

²⁷ Then He looked right straight at Thomas and said, *"Howdy Thomas, look here at My hands. You can touch them with your fingers, and put your hand here in My side. I don't want ya to be doubtin' no more pardner, but start believin'."*

²⁸ Well, Thomas didn't need to do any of that stuff, no-sir-ee. He fell right down on his knees sayin', "My Lord and My God!"

²⁹ Jesus said to him, *"Is it 'cause you've seen Me you believe? Blessed are the folks who don't see Me but still believe."*

³⁰ Now there's a whole lot more signs and miracles Jesus did when He was with His pardners that ain't wrote down in this book.

³¹ But these here are a handful of 'em kept in this record so y'all might each one believe that Jesus is the Messiah, the Son of God, and by believin' you can have everlastin' life in His name.

Thinkin' Questions

1. If you are a believer, you have also received the Holy Spirit as Jesus promised. When and where did you first believe and trust Jesus as your Savior?

2. Has there ever been a time when you felt like you had lost your faith and later had it renewed by an encounter with the Lord? Describe that time in your life.

∞℃

The Good Book records 13 resurrection appearances of Jesus:

1. At the empty tomb on Resurrection Sunday – Matthew 28:1-8; Mark 16:1-8 and Luke 24:1-12.
2. To Mary Magdalene on Resurrection Sunday in the garden at the tomb – Mark 16:9-11 and John 20:1-17.
3. To some other women on Resurrection Sunday – Matthew 28:9-10.
4. To two disciples on the road to Emmaus on Resurrection Sunday – Mark 16:12-13 and Luke 24:13-32.
5. To Peter in Jerusalem on Resurrection Sunday – Luke 24:34 and I Corinthians 15:5.
6. To the ten disciples in the Upper Room in Jerusalem on Resurrection Sunday (Thomas is absent) – Luke 24:36-43 and John 20:19-25.
7. To the eleven disciples in the Upper Room in Jerusalem the following Sunday (Thomas is present) – Mark 16:14; John 20:26-31 and I Corinthians 15:5.
8. To seven disciples fishing on the Sea of Galilee – John 21:1-14.
9. To the eleven disciples on a mountain in Galilee – Matthew 28:16-20 and Mark 16:15-18.
10. To more than 500 believers at one time – I Corinthians 15:6.
11. To James His half-brother and author of the Epistle of James – I Corinthians 15:7.
12. To the disciples at His ascension on the Mt. of Olives 40 days after His resurrection – Luke 24:44-49 and Acts 1:3-9.
13. To Paul on the road to Damascus several years later – Acts 9:1-19; Acts 22:3-16; Acts 26:9-18 and I Corinthians 9:1.

∞℃

Chapter Twenty-one

Campfire by the Sea

Chapter Twenty-one – Campfire by the Sea

¹ After a spell Jesus appeared to His pardners again by the Sea of Galilee, and here's how it all came about:

²⁻³ One evenin' some of Jesus' pardners and friends was hangin' out together there by the seashore. It was ol' Peter, with Thomas the twin, and Nathanael who was from over in Cana in Galilee and them parts. There was Zebedee's two sons and a couple of other pardners there. Peter spoke up and said, "I don't know about y'all fellas, but I'm goin' fishin'." And they all said, "Wait up, we're goin' with ya." So they all got into a fishin' boat to do some serious fishin'. Well, turns out they fished all night and never got a nibble.

⁴ Now just at the break of dawn Jesus was standin' on the shore, but the pardners hadn't any notion it was Him.

⁵ Jesus hollered out to 'em, *"Howdy boys, y'all caught anything?"* And they answered back, "Nope, nothin' all night!"

⁶ So He shouted back to 'em, *"Go ahead and toss your net on the right side of your boat out there and y'all just might find a catch of fish!"* Well, why not? So they cast the net where He told 'em and there was so many fish they couldn't even pull the net back up in the boat.

⁷ Then the pardner that Jesus rightly favored recognized Him and told Peter, "Hey Peter, it's the Boss!" When Peter heard that it was the Lord, he quick put on his shirt and jumped right off the boat into the water and started swimmin' for the shore where Jesus was.

⁸ The other pardners stayed in the boat and here they all come a-rowin' to shore draggin' that net full of fish behind 'em. They weren't far out, only about 100 yards.

⁹ When they got on shore, they saw a campfire was a-goin' with some fish cookin' on it already, and there was some biscuits too.

¹⁰ Jesus said to 'em, *"Bring some of the fish over here that y'all caught."*

Thinkin' Questions

1. Jesus appeared to the disciples one early morning after an unsuccessful night of fishing. Study the scene in **verses 1-10.** List things Jesus knew and ways He met their needs in a real way that morning. Apply these to your own life.

<u>Things Jesus knew</u>   <u>Ways Jesus met their needs</u>

_____   _____

_____   _____

_____   _____

[11] Peter went and pulled the net up on the land and it was plumb full of big fish —a hundred and fifty-three he counted, yes-sir-ee. A catch that size should've busted the net, but don't ya know the net weren't even torn.

[12-13] Jesus said, *"Come on fellas, let's eat breakfast."* None of His pardners asked Him, "Who are You?" 'cause they all done reckoned it was the Lord Himself. Jesus served up vittles and biscuits and they all ate.

[14] Now this was the third time that Jesus done showed Hisself to His pardners since He had been raised from the dead.

[15] After they had done finished eatin' breakfast, Jesus said to Simon Peter, *"Simon, son of John, do you love Me more than these other pardners?"* "Yep, I sure do," Peter said, "You know I'm Your sidekick." *"Then feed My lambs,"* Jesus told him.

[16] After a little while, Jesus asked the question again: *"Simon, son of John, do you really love Me?"* "Ya know I rightly do, Boss" Peter said. Jesus said to him, *"Then watch over My sheep."*

[17] One more time the Lord asked him, *"Simon, son of John, do you love Me?"* Well Peter was right disappointed 'cause Jesus done asked him the third time, *"Do ya love Me?"* Peter answered Him again, "Lord You know everything and You know what's in my heart; You know that I love ya and I'm true now for sure." So Jesus said to him, *"Feed My little lambs."*

[18] *"I'm tellin' ya straight Peter, when you were younger you could buckle on your own belt and ride whatever trail ya wanted. But … when you're old, you will stretch out your hands and other fellas will buckle you up and lead ya down a trail you plumb don't wanna go down."*

[19] Now Jesus said this thing to Peter lettin' him know the way his days would come to an end; and how by his death he would glorify God. After that Jesus said to Peter, *"Follow Me."*

Thinkin' Questions

1. What past events prompted the Lord Jesus to deal with Peter in such a way asking him the same question three times? **Read Matthew 26:33-35 & 69-75.**

2. We know that Peter was fully restored as an apostle and leader of the early church. What does this say to us about our failures as believers? **Refer to James 4:6-10 and 1 John 1:8-9.**

3. Peter went through much testing recorded in Scripture. From sinking in waves to the crucifixion of Christ and beyond. According to **verse 18**, does the testing of Peter's faith ever stop?

4. The key for getting through our own struggles is found in **verse 19**: *"After that Jesus said to Peter, "*_____ _____.*"*

Chapter 21　　　　　　　　　　　Just Thinkin

In life experiences the easy path is to always return to our comfort zone. Our tendency is to do that which we know and are comfortable in doing. It's like a young drover always picking up the drag because that's what he knows. What if his trail boss told him to ride swing instead? Our Christian walk is no exception. Ya see, that's what Peter did (after the death and resurrection of Jesus). He went back to doing what he knew best; back to his comfort zone – "Peter spoke up and said, 'I don't know about y'all fellas, but I'm goin' fishin'" (John 21:3). But Jesus had other plans for Peter, not to go fishing for fish but to become a fisherman of men (Matthew 5:19). In Jesus' conversation with Peter in verses 15-17, He says to Peter three times to leave off fishing and to feed and tend His sheep.

As born again Christians, the Lord has also given us an assignment, even as He did Peter. To do so may require us to step out of our comfort zone. However we can know that He will always ride the trail with us as our faithful pardner. *"I reckon to ask the Father, He'll send along to you another Trail Guide who will ride the trail with each of you forever. I'm talkin' about the Spirit of truth. The folks of this world won't let Him in, 'cause they can't see Him and don't know Him. But y'all know Him 'cause He'll be ridin' alongside you and will for sure be in you"* (John 14:16-17).

²⁰ And while they was walkin' along and talkin' a bit more, Peter looked around and saw the young pardner Jesus was particular fond of followin' along after 'em. It was the same one that done leaned in close at the supper and asked Jesus, "Who is it, Lord?" when they found out one of 'em was gonna turn against Him.

²¹ So when Peter spotted him, he said to Jesus, "And what about this fella, Lord?"

²² Jesus told Peter, *"If I want him to stay on here 'til I come back again, what's that to you? It's up to you to follow Me."*

²³ Now because of what Jesus said, it was spread through the whole outfit that this pardner would not die. But Jesus never said to him that he wouldn't die. What He did say was, *"If I want him to stay on here 'til I come back again, what's that to you?"*

²⁴ It's that very pardner who is testifyin' to all these things, and done wrote these things down. And we all know that his testimony is true.

²⁵ But this ain't a drop in the bucket of all the things that Jesus did when He walked this earth. If it was all wrote down, and the details of it; well I guess that even the world itself wouldn't be big enough to hold all the books that could be written about Jesus.

Thinkin' Questions

1. Jesus is letting Peter know in **verse 23** that God's plan for his life is personal for him as an individual. What does this say to us about comparisons and speculations of another believer's journey? **Read Romans 14:12-13 and James 4:11-12.**

2. In your own heart and mind, spend some time with the Lord Jesus around His campfire. Talk and listen to Him about His plan for your life. Confess as needed the things that are wrong in your life. Trust Him anew for the future and then commit to get on the trail He has for you personally. Record your thoughts below and any Scriptures He brings to mind. Date and initial your notes.

The authors of this Bible Study pray for you as you ride the trail with the Lord.

Ridin' the Trail With Jesus

In case you've been on the wrong trail, and thinkin' maybe it's too late or you don't know how to get on the RIGHT one, God has good news for you. He wants you to ride through life with Him through His Son, Jesus Christ. He has an amazing destination in mind for you at the end of the trail. You can ride right along with Jesus through this life all the way to life everlasting in the great beyond.

The Bible says . . .
"For God so loved the world, that He gave His only begotten Son, that whoever believes in Him shall not perish, but have eternal life." *John 3:16*

The problem is us! Every one of us tends to stray. The Good Book calls it sin. The first man and woman sinned. They made a willful choice to disobey God and to ride their own trail. We still do that today. Sin results in separation from God. It fences us out of His presence.

The Bible says . . .
"For all have sinned and fall short of the glory of God." *Romans 3:23*

It also says . . .
"For the wages of sin is death." *Romans 6:23a*

Most of us think that we can find our own way to God and heaven. We think that we can lift ourselves up by our own bootstraps. If I am good enough . . . If I do enough good works . . . If the good outweighs the bad . . . I do deserve heaven, don't I? God says there is only one way to heaven; only one gate through which we can enter.

The Bible says . . .
Jesus said, "I am the way, and the truth, and the life; no one comes to the Father but through Me." John 14:6

Jesus is the only way back to God through the endless fences built by our sin. He is the only 'perfect' man who has ever lived; the sinless Son of God. He took our place and died on the cross and rose from the grave so that our sins can be forgiven and taken out of the way. He opened up the only gate in the fence. He is the gate.

The Bible says . . .
"But God demonstrates His own love toward us, in that while we were yet sinners, Christ died for us . . . the free gift of God is eternal life in Christ Jesus our Lord." Romans 5:8, 6:23b

We must choose whether we want to ride the trail with Jesus to life everlasting or ride our own trail that leads to destruction.

The Bible says . . .
"There is a way *which seems* right to a man, but its end is the way of death." Proverbs 14:12

You can decide to ride with Jesus by trusting Him to be your Lord and Savior.

Next. . .
The Bible says . . .
". . . if you confess with your mouth Jesus as Lord, and believe in your heart that God raised Him from the dead, you will be saved; for with the heart a person believes, resulting in righteousness, and with the mouth he confesses, resulting in salvation. . . . for 'Whoever will call on the name of the LORD will be saved.'" Romans 10:9-10, 13

"Whoever believes in Him (Jesus) shall not perish, but have eternal life." John 3:16

Which trail will you ride into eternity? Will you receive Jesus right now as Savior and trust Him alone as your riding partner to life everlasting? If so, admit to God that you are a sinner. Ask Him to forgive you, leaving all other trails behind to ride the one trail with Jesus. Believe that Jesus died on the cross and rose from the grave to take away your sin. Accept Jesus' offer of salvation and ask Him to come into your heart and life.

You might say a prayer something like this:
Dear Jesus, thank you for making it possible for me to ride the trail of life with You. I admit that I have made a wreck of my life; that I have tried to ride my own trail. I believe You died on the cross to pay the penalty for my sins and rose to life again so I can live forever. I'm askin' You, Lord, to forgive my sins and come into my heart. I want to ride the trail of life with You beginning this very moment and ride with You into life everlasting. Amen.

*All scriptures quoted in "Ridin' the Trail With Jesus" are taken from the *New American Standard Bible*

Printed in the United States
By Bookmasters